FIRED-UP FULFILLED AND FREE

KNOW WHO YOU ARE. GET OUT OF YOUR OWN WAY. LIVE YOUR PURPOSE.

JULI WENGER

Dedication

This book is dedicated to my army. To the collection of people that have supported and encouraged my journey into becoming an author. To everyone who God has sent alongside me to remind me who I am, thank you.

To my husband, Dustin, thank you for believing in me before I believed in myself.

To my children, Jackson, Kennedy, and Ceili, you inspire me to be a better mom, a better person, and to leave the world more filled with love.

Mom and Dad, thank you for raising me surrounded by faith.

To my brothers and sisters in Jesus, my writing accountability group, my coaches, my clients, and every friend who has seen beyond my playing small stories, thank you for calling me up.

And to my Father, my Savior, my Healer, and my Provider, thank you for calling me to this path. I am blessed and grateful.

Disclaimer

While the stories in this book are true, some names and identifying information may have been changed or combined to protect the privacy of individuals.

This book contains advice and information relating to health and personal wellness. It is not intended to replace medical advice, or the recommendation of your psychologist, therapist, or other mental health professionals. All efforts have been made to assure the accuracy of the information contained in this book as of the date of publication. The publisher and author disclaim liability for any medical or psychological outcomes that may occur as a result of applying the methods suggested in this book.

While the author has made every effort to provide accurate internet addresses at the time of publication, neither the publisher nor the author assumes any responsibility for errors or for changes that occur after publication. Further, the author does not have any control over and does not assume any responsibility for third-party websites or their content.

TABLE OF CONTENTS

CHAPTER ONE

THE JOURNEY

PART ONE: CALLING YOU UP

"Belonging doesn't come from outside of you.
It's an inside job."

This book is a call. A shout from the rooftops. An invitation. The words you're about to read have been lovingly written for you. To shake you out of your settling. To shake you out of your commitment to not-enoughness. To shake you out of your need for certainty. To remind you who you are. And to help you get clear on why you're here.

I've been in that place of not knowing. Wondering if the life I was living mattered and if all the hard work I was putting into building it was worth the effort. I have lived in the illusion that I was defined by my achievements, certifications and training, and titles and roles. My life was defined by shrinking and playing small, merging with other people's opinions and "shoulds," waiting for perfect and hiding my light. I spent so long not allowing myself to show up or shine because I was scared of not being enough. I was scared of being rejected. I was scared of being unlovable. I spent so much of my life searching for affirmation outside of myself, searching for belonging. And in that search, I lost who I was. When we lose who we are, we belong nowhere.

Little did I know, the only reason I didn't belong somewhere was because I was so caught up in my belief that I wasn't enough that I didn't allow myself to belong. I didn't believe I was worthy, so I actively created not belonging. I blocked it. I was looking for my needs to be met outside of myself. I was looking to others to tell me that I was enough. I was looking to others to tell me that I was loveable. I was looking to others to tell me that I was worthy. But even if they did, I couldn't receive it.

Here's the hard truth, belonging doesn't come from outside of you. It's an inside job. And the work is to understand and accept that belonging exists in the relationship with a God who created you to belong to Him. A Father who says, "Hey! I've got you. Don't you trust me yet? Haven't I always shown up for you and had your back?" He's a God inviting you to go on one wild and crazy ride back to who you are. He's inviting you into life beyond fear, into a FIRED-UP, FULFILLED, and FREE life.

You're reading this book because He's calling you to it. It's time to get out of your way. It's time to learn what He has for planned you. It's time to stop hiding. It's time for faith. And it's time to give an honest answer to the question, "Do you trust Me yet?" Maybe it's a "no." Maybe it's that you want to, or you know you should. But if you're really owning where you stand, the answer is "not yet." Or "sometimes." Or "that depends." Or "I'm learning to." Regardless of where you are in this journey of trusting Him, you are being called back to yourself, called to be an authentic, powerful, bold, and unapologetic you.

Welcome to the journey, my loves. Let go of the idea that it's going to be smooth sailing from here on out—you're going to battle. It's your moment to face fear. It's your moment to let go of old patterns that no longer serve you. It's time to step into the power placed in you and create the impact in this world that only you can. It's time for courage, confidence, and clarity. And I'm here to hold your hand as you step through fear to live in the freedom that is your birthright as a child of God.

Are you ready for His call? Repeat after me.

I am here on purpose, with purpose, and for purpose.
I am wrapped in strength, might, and power.
I will not be burned by the fire because in me is God, and He is the ultimate all-consuming fire.
I will be the light in the night.
I have been given power and authority greater than what's in this world.
I claim joy.
I claim peace.
I claim wholeness.
I laugh in the face of fear.
I am created for a moment such as this—this exact moment.
And I will not be moved.
The call on my life is greater than I can imagine, control, or plan on my own and I allow myself to surrender to the beautiful plan of my God who loves me fiercely.

It's go-time.

PART TWO: A FEAR TO FREEDOM FOUNDATION

"The way to freedom is through faith, and faith allows us to step through fear."

Let's start with some foundation that we can build on. How much fear is in your life? As far back as I can remember, fear was my companion. I was afraid that I wasn't enough. I was afraid that I would fail. I was afraid that I would be rejected or judged. I was afraid that I'd never measure up to who I was supposed to be. Fear was always all around me. And yet, I've come to realize, after stepping through a lot of fear, that it's normal. Fear is the ONE thing that keeps us all stuck. How it shows up may vary, but we all have it. It's hardwired into us.

I took on an exercise once that brought a lot of clarity to this. I was about a year into a new business, and I was working on marketing messaging. Trying to get clear on what exactly it was that I do. I knew I was seeing massive transformation in people, but how could I describe it? I polled clients. I read testimonials. I brainstormed on a giant whiteboard. And then, I went to dig through client notes. That's where the gold was. What was it that they were coming to me with? What was it that they were struggling with? As I started reading through all these notes, I was struck by how much variety there seemed to be in the "pain points" that people were showing up to overcome. I started to write them down with a sharpie on bright blue sticky notes—each new pain point got its own sticky note and then was placed on the wall beside my desk. When I was done, I stood back and looked at the wall with more than 200 sticky notes.

More than 200 pain points, including each of these (grab a pen or a highlighter and make a list of any of these that you identify with):

- Insecurity
- Rejection
- Failure
- Abandonment
- Overwhelm
- Worry about disappointing people
- Worry about being discovered as a fraud
- Worry about being unlovable
- Not trusting myself
- Not trusting other people
- Not being in control of my own life
- Worry about being judged
- Feeling scared of success
- Not wanting to be taken advantage of
- Feeling unsafe
- Feeling unprotected
- Not knowing how to say no
- Overachieving to the point of burnout
- Perfectionism
- Comparison
- Co-dependency
- An inability to celebrate myself or others
- Avoidance
- Procrastination
- Humility to the point of hiding
- Aiming for success by other people's standards
- Being too busy

- Being a control freak
- Exhaustion
- Self-sabotage
- Being too loyal
- An inability to cope
- Questioning my value

That's just a few of them! I felt the immense weight of all the challenges that these people, who I loved and was journeying with, were encountering. I felt the weight of the struggles they faced. I stared at that wall and wondered, "What ties it all together? Can I categorize it? They must be linked somehow..." And then, I had my light-bulb moment—they are all driven by FEAR. The core of every single pain point was fear. We all need to feel safe and loved, but fear tells us that those needs for safety and love won't be met. Fear tells us that we are incapable or unworthy of having our needs met, so we create stories and behavior patterns to try to meet those needs ourselves, which often results in some combination of challenges on this list.

This wasn't just heavy. It was also powerful because I had seen these same people journey through fear. They were each on a path of taking their power back and learning to love themselves.

I had seen people struggling with a complete lack of self-love and boundaries learn to ask for what they need and say no to what wasn't serving them and their purpose. I had walked alongside people who were burnt out as they learned to take care of themselves. I'd watched people who hated their jobs create new opportunities, start new businesses, and completely redefine success.

I got curious – if fear was the common denominator of these pain points and struggles, what was the common denominator on the other side of the journey? So, I did what I always do—I made more sticky notes. I went back through each notebook, looking for the wins and reflecting on the changes I saw in each of these incredible people on their journeys back to themselves. Transformations like: (Pull out your pen or highlighter again – which of these are what you want?)

- Learning to believe in myself
- Creating clear direction
- Owning my needs
- Finding balance and harmony
- Loving myself
- Feeling empowered
- Experiencing peace
- Feeling safe
- Finding flow
- Living in alignment and integrity with myself and God
- Learning to trust myself
- Finding real excitement for life
- Experiencing personal growth and expansion
- Having clarity of purpose for my life
- Living in a state of joy
- Living with permission to be authentically me
- Experiencing fearless confidence
- Finding my motivation

Do you know what all of that is? Do you see the common theme? It's FREEDOM! On the other side of fear is freedom. This was it. The other side of the journey, the other side of the growth, all amounted to freedom. And this was what God had taken me through. My own fear-to-freedom journey. He'd walked me out of being overwhelmed and into a space where I could breathe again. He'd taken me through a process of letting go of my commitments to being busy, worrying, and continually looking for my shortcomings so that I could experience peace, fulfillment, and sustainable joy. He'd brought me into freedom. Galatians 5:1 (NIV) says, "It is for freedom that Christ has set us free. Stand firm, then, and do not let yourselves be burdened again by a yoke of slavery." Freedom is what He wanted for me. It's what He wants for you too.

In this book, I'm going to guide you through your journey from fear to freedom. I'll walk you through what God took me through. Your fear has kept you stuck, but no longer. It's time to stand firm and throw off the burden of fear. The way to freedom is through faith, and faith allows us to step through fear. It allows us to cast it out and remember who we are. It allows us to fully claim our birthright as sons and daughters. "For God has not given us a spirit of fear and timidity, but of power, love, and self-discipline" (2 Timothy 1:7).

So, buckle up because we're going to start at the heart of one of the biggest fears out there—am I enough?

CHAPTER TWO

THE ENOUGHNESS ILLUSION

PART ONE: "AM I ENOUGH?"

"We lose touch with ourselves because we've attached our identity to what we perceive "enoughness" to be."

It's the question that crosses all the divides: gender, race, and socio-economic status. It crosses oceans and stretches through centuries. "Am I enough?" shows up for everyone. No one is exempt. Even me! It's the question that has underpinned my entire life—so far. It's driven my patterns of playing small, questioning my value, and proving my worth. "Am I enough?"

There is often a qualifier that shows up in this statement too. "Am I [fill-in-the-blank] enough?" Think about that for a minute. What comes to mind for you? What are the obvious areas where you struggle or believe you're not enough? Write them down. What are the less obvious areas? Write those down too.

If you need some ideas (though I can guarantee that you don't), here's my list:

Am I...
- Pretty enough
- Skinny enough
- Tall enough
- Smart enough
- Blonde enough

- Entrepreneurial enough
- Business-minded enough
- Healthy enough
- A good enough mother, wife, daughter, sister, Christian, ally, activist, housekeeper, coach, podcaster, friend, aunt, cousin, singer, songwriter, author, teacher.... Hmmm... what else...
- Stylish enough
- Rich enough
- Humble enough
- Quiet enough
- Loud enough
- Modest enough
- Confident enough
- Focused enough
- Creative enough
- Detailed enough
- Visionary enough

Ok, I'm going to stop there. I could go on and on and on. But you get the point. We carry so many expectations. There are so many areas where we can compare and contrast ourselves to some societal or cultural standard. It's a losing battle. Look at this list—or even better, your list. Where do these standards and expectations even come from? When you read your list, whose voice do you hear? Take a minute and get curious – do you have an idea of where or who your "not enough" stories came from? And is it even humanly possible to be "enough" in all those areas at the same time? There are opposites in that list. What I see here is that for one of these expectations to be true and me to be enough in one area, by default, would mean that I'm not enough in another. How can I manage to be both loud enough and quiet enough at the same time? How do I create a circumstance where I can meet all the expectations in all the areas at once? Are you exhausted just looking at this? I sure am.

"Enoughness" is exhausting. We spend so much time and energy spiraling in this question, looking at it in multiple contexts and often all simultaneously—hands up if you're with me— that we lose ourselves in the swirl of not measuring up.

When I say we lose ourselves, I don't just mean in the context of a momentary loss of self when we can't tell which way is up. I also mean a disconnect with the bigger picture—who we are at our core. We actually forget who we are. We can get so lost in trying to be enough as a parent or enough as a partner or enough as a boss or enough as an employee (fill in your list here) that we start to think that who we are is directly tied to our success or failure in those spaces. We lose touch with ourselves because we've attached our identity to what we perceive "enoughness" to be.

PART TWO: THE SOURCE OF NOT-ENOUGHNESS

"We are taught that our measuring up to society's standards is the source of our worthiness."

Where did it all start anyway? I don't have a childhood filled with big traumas. There are no defining moments in my memory or early life that would have caused me to start filtering myself for common consumption and acceptance. There were no major events that led to me trying to be enough. No triggers that threw me into a pattern of proving or adapting to who I thought I needed to be. That came later. Little me experienced what I can only explain as a slow building-up of armor as I interacted with a broken world. Like all kids, I was trying to find my way, and, true to my brain structure at the time, I was experiencing EVERYTHING with the belief that everything revolved around me. In the field of psychology, this is often referred to as healthy or essential narcissism, which was introduced through the work of Heinz Kohut. In the context of childhood development, healthy narcissism functions to support the development of our sense of self [1].

Essential narcissism is a normal part of the process of defining our identity. And that meant little Juli perceived all the things that seemed to go wrong around her or for people around her as a "ME THING." My fault, my lack, my failure. If I could just be better, then things would be better.

Likely my not-enoughness was also significantly impacted by shame culture. I distinctly remember listening to the audiobook of Daring Greatly while driving home from work one day and hearing Brené Brown talk about the difference between shame and guilt.

"Shame is the intensely painful feeling or experience of believing that we are flawed and therefore unworthy of love or belonging." [2] It is an identification of self as good or bad. I AM good, or I AM bad. Versus guilt that is more about "I made a poor choice" or "I made a good choice" and knowing that they don't reflect on me as a person [3]. The difference is knowing that my poor choices or good choices don't fundamentally define who I am. They don't require me to change how I perceive myself. This was a true "pull the car over" moment as the context of my childhood experience and my parents' experience, and their parents' experience came flooding in.

I thought of how my grandparents expected everything to be "just so" and how when we would visit, we'd hug them and then disappear to the basement, where we would largely be unseen and unheard. I thought of how I wasn't allowed to get my ears pieced for years because it was "of the devil." How the house had to look a certain way to avoid judgment. There was a generational pattern of measuring up and "being good" or "being enough." There was a black and white context of whether you're good or not. Either you're worthy of love, or you're not. Either you measure up, or you don't. I also started to understand that everyone had done the best they could with what they had been taught. How they had been taught to think about themselves and judge themselves and others. How they had been taught to discipline children. How they had been taught to worry about what people think. It was no wonder that I was so convinced that I wasn't enough—I'd been brought up with a story that my failures and successes define my value, and my measuring up determined my enoughness.

This is bred into us! We are taught that our measuring up to society's standards is the source of our worthiness.

Can we pause here for a minute? Read that again.

We are taught that our measuring up to society's standards is the source of our worthiness.

This is such a big issue in western society. For example, we compare ourselves to supermodels. We are incessantly flooded with images and advertising that tell us who we are meant to be from when we are little. As a mom, this is terrifying. Looking back to little Juli, I can see it so clearly. I had mirrored closet doors in my bedroom, the sliding kind that nest behind each other, and they became my judgment screen. I'd stand in front of them on my tiptoes, suck in my tummy, and stick my chest out to see how closely I could imitate Barbie, a Disney Princess, Christina Aguilera, or whoever my most current model of beauty was. As I got older, I'd practice singing and dancing in front of those doors, choreographing moves to every Backstreet Boys song, wondering if I was talented enough to give Britney Spears a run for her money.

It sounds amusing, but there was a deeper and more insidious thread in all of this. I'd bought into the societal narrative of what pretty, popular, and good enough looked and sounded like. I was developing a pattern of evaluating myself through that lens, looking for my worth outside of myself, and managing perceptions.

At school, I was the awkward try-too-hard kid. I wanted so much to be popular because that's what enoughness looked like, right? I was so focused on fitting in that I sabotaged the very thing I wanted. I became too awkward to fit in and too talkative to be cool. I didn't have the Nike shoes, the Adidas sweatshirt, or the trendy dresses, and I thought that defined me. Not enough? Checkmark.

Plus, we were the family that was always at church. Music practice, leadership meetings, improvement projects... you name it, and we were there. It was like a second home. But did I belong there? Nope. My awkward try-too-hard self showed up there too, desperately wanting to be enough somewhere and to be the one that all the other kids were excited to see. But my experience, instead, was of exclusion. Not enough? Another checkmark.

Quick sidebar—and this is important to share here—I had parents who loved each other and their kids. We were a nuclear family in a time when that was still the average dynamic. I was the oldest of three kids with two younger brothers. We had a warm home, good food to eat, a swing set in the backyard, and a raspberry patch you could play hide-and-seek in. We lived in a safe neighborhood and walked to school every day through an apple orchard. We didn't have loads of money, but we had enough. We camped every summer. We watched cartoons on Saturday morning and Disney movies on Sunday nights. Life was good. And yet, not enough? Checkmark.

Not-enoughness lives outside of family dynamics and lifestyle. Not-enoughness is not about rich or poor, stable, or chaotic, healthy or unhealthy. Not-enoughness is pervasive. It's an attack on identity. It's part of the human condition. And it's an illusion.

Yup, I've lived my whole life struggling with "Am I enough?" and I am telling you that it is a complete and utter load of crap. It's an illusion of the subconscious mind. It's a story meant to keep us safe. It serves a purpose, and we're going to talk about that. But it doesn't exist.

We live in an epidemic of not-enoughness, and it's rooted in our culture. A shame culture. A society devoted to polarities. Good versus bad. Fat versus skinny. Success versus failure. Black vs. white. Enough versus not enough. In God's eyes, though, none of this is relevant. All this comparison and jealousy throws us into a shame spiral and takes us out of alignment with Him. He wants us to be love, and we have to start with being love to ourselves. We cannot give love and be love if we aren't operating that way with ourselves. We'd just be faking it.

PART THREE: WHAT'S ENOUGH ANYWAY?

"You are enough because you are chosen."

You're probably having one of the two possible reactions right now. There's relief and the head nod. A "Yeah, that makes sense that enoughness is an illusion." Or there is a tension that resembles an argument. You're ready to fight because enoughness is no illusion. It's real! It's defined your whole freaking life so far. Well, wave hello to your ego, take a deep breath, and stay with me.

Let's take a minute and think about this. What is enough? Go ahead, map it out. Is there actually a place you can reach where you would finally and fully be enough? Or is it a moving target? I'll wait.

When I ask this question, "moving target" is the answer 100 percent of the time. I've never seen an exception. We are all flawed human beings. We are broken. We will never measure up. But He who is in us, He is enough. He is perfect. Jesus covers all of it. And here's the deal. HE DECIDED TO CALL ON YOU, TO CREATE YOU, TO LOVE YOU. Come on now! We skip over this stuff, but you need to take a breath and be receptive here. Don't miss this! Slow down and tune in. You are enough because you are made with purpose. You are enough because the Maker of the universe decided the world needed you. You are enough because He has placed a calling on your life. You are enough because you are chosen. You are enough because He loves you.

The only one who can define and obtain enoughness is the Creator of all things. That creation just happens to include you. Wonderfully made you. WONDER-FULL. Buying into the story that you're not enough contradicts God's plan and purpose for you. You buying into the story that you're not enough is like saying God got it wrong. Are you perfect? No! But HE makes you worthy. And His grace covers everything.

Look, I get it. I've chosen to operate as though I know better than Him. I've chosen to live in a state of believing that I am outside of the bounds of His grace. I've chosen to try to figure life out and build success and fulfillment on my own. But it never seems to work out the way I hoped.

CHAPTER THREE

RECLAIMING ENOUGH

PART ONE: YOUR ENOUGHNESS IS SETTLED

"Your enoughness does not live within other's perceptions."

YOU ARE ENOUGH BECAUSE YOU EXIST. Read that again. You are enough because you exist.

The only way you become not enough is if you choose it. Your enoughness is settled unless you unsettle it. Which means you have a choice to make. Will you continue to operate from a fundamentally untrue and flawed story that contradicts who God says you are? Or will you claim what's already in you and allow Him to work through you? Will you allow God your Father to bring you back to who He created you to be? Will you claim the peace of mind and heart you've been promised as a gift? (John 14:27) A gift! We don't earn gifts, we receive them.

Test this statement out with me: "I AM ENOUGH. MY ENOUGHNESS IS SETTLED."

I remember hearing this and initially not getting it. I thought that maybe when I got a little closer to enoughness, I would be able to accept that my enoughness was settled. Sound familiar? When I'm more worthy, then I can reach toward believing that my enoughness is settled. When people see me a certain way, when they tell me I've reached the point I'm striving for, when I'm successful, then maybe, just maybe, I can be enough.

Understand this. That's all a load of crap. Giving your power to everyone else's expectations is what has you in this space of "I'm not enough" in the first place. Striving for someone else's bar, reaching for and trying to prove that you can look a certain way, sound a certain way, walk a certain way, angle your face or flip your hair a certain way, or make a certain amount of money is all for validation from outside of yourself. It's all for outside affirmation that you're enough. Here's the issue: Your enoughness does not live within others' perceptions. Or your perceptions of their perceptions. Do you really know what they think anyway? It is more common that you make up a story about not-enoughness because you bought into your personal perception of what other people think you should be, and you're gauging your perception of their responses. I know that's a lot of perceptions, but that's exactly the point. What you have taken on as reality probably isn't. Stop it already.

Let's go back to the basis of our faith. Your enoughness is settled because Jesus bled out on a cross for you. If that sounds harsh, good. It was. He loves you that much. With all your shortcomings, He loves you anyway. With all your imperfections, He loves you anyway. There is nothing you can do and nowhere you can go to make Him love you any less. He wants you free of this enoughness nonsense. Which means you get to make a choice.

PART TWO: IT'S A CHOICE

"Not-enoughness is not something that I can magically let go of, but enoughness is something I can actively choose."

Let's talk about choice, shall we? A few years ago, I went to a "woo-woo" retreat. For those of you who are wondering what "woo-woo" is, it's my definition of societal spirituality that isn't founded in following Jesus. That's a whole story in and of itself but suffice it to say that God can work through any circumstance, and He showed up powerfully in this one. My intention for going on this retreat, which involved flying to a different country and leaving my small children for the first time, was to let go of my fear of not being enough. Yup, true story.

I had realized that the fear of not being enough was driving my entire life. It clouded all my decisions. I was people-pleasing so hard that I'd practically wrung myself inside out trying to make everyone happy while finding some version of success in the process. And it was working, which was a testament to how much I was giving to my business and to every space I was operating in and how little I was giving to myself. I was burnt out, and I had completely hit my wall. I was carrying EVERYTHING I could get my hands on—everyone's expectations, happiness, emotions, challenges, you name it. I placed it all on my shoulders, day after day after day.

So, I got on a plane, flew to Oregon, drove up to wine country, and knew that this would be the transformation of my life. On day one, I walked into the event space, and the tears began. All the overwhelm. All the fear. All the frustration. All the sadness. All the anger. All the worry. All the carrying. It fell out of me. For two days, my head pounded with one of the worst headaches of my life, but my heart was so full of emotion I hadn't let myself feel that I couldn't contain it anymore. This safe space where I didn't need to be anything for anyone was an outlet I could finally take advantage of. It was a space where I could slow down my busy life enough for a giant pattern interrupt.

After two days of tears and a next-level blotchy, red-crying face, we shifted from processing what was bottled up to rebuilding. Day three was when we looked at two of the three major emotions we were there to rewire, sadness and anger. We looked for where those emotions first showed up for us. We meditated on them, and God showed up with me. The meditation process was to drift up out of your body and take someone with you if you wanted, which had me in "I'm going to take the Holy Spirit with me because I don't know how I feel about all this woo going on up in here." Then we would go back to the moment when anger or sadness first showed up, and we would look for the learning opportunity, the gift, or how it shaped us. We would then thank the circumstance, which effectively re-framed how we saw or experienced it, and that would (in theory) change our perspective moving forward. Essentially it was a gratitude practice. Each time, I'd say, "Ok, Holy Spirit, use this." And each time, there was a lesson. It felt freeing. It felt grounding. I felt so much more connected to myself and my faith. The whole time God reminded me of who I was and how He saw me. I felt especially hopeful because day four was fear day. I naively thought, "This is it. I'm going to conquer this enoughness thing once and for all, and then I'll be unstoppable."

Side note number one: I didn't realize this at the time, but this is NOT how the growth journey works. The growth journey happens in layers. It takes time. It requires us to do work. It requires coming back to ourselves. It's a partnership with God that brings us back to Him at the same time. It's not a "do one woo-woo meditation and you're cured" thing.

Side note number two: It's not lost on me that I was still trying to do everything myself. I was still in control mode, and surrender was not in my vocabulary.

Anyway, I stepped into day four with all kinds of fire and hope. "Bring it!" We settled in to do the first of two fear meditations. We started with a reflection to explore where fear first showed up. "Ok, Holy Spirit, let's do this." And we did. It was one of the most transformational moments of my life so far. I had a vision of floating up and up and up, and eventually, I was dancing in space with the Holy Spirit, swaying back and forth, feeling peaceful. Our facilitator indicated that we were going back in time to revisit the first moment of fear, but unlike when we were exploring sadness and anger, there was no change for me. Outside of time, I was hanging out with God, swaying back and forth and looking down on the earth. Content. Calm. I looked at the world and heard as clear as day, "These are my children who I love." At that moment, I knew that my life was about something so much bigger than me and my experience, and it didn't require me to go back in time to root out fear. Fear wasn't mine. There was nothing to re-frame or take power away from because there is no fear in HIM. Because "perfect love drives out fear" (1 John 4:18, NIV). He showed me that I had given my power to something that never deserved it, and it was time to take it back.

I knew that God was giving me clarity on my purpose too. He was calling me at that moment. "Go love my children." We came back out of the meditation, and I was over the moon. I thought, "Let's do the second one so I can go thank fear for not being mine and ditch not-enoughness." I still thought they were inextricably tied. I believed that I was almost there. Almost free of this nonsense that had been holding me down. I thought, "Imagine what I can do if I'm not afraid of not being enough!"

Well, here's the twist. We started the second meditation, and I was completely stuck in my body. I was going nowhere. "I'm sorry God, what?" And as I was stuck, all I could see was light and darkness on the horizon in my mind and clouds in front that seemed to be masking a battle. Two things struck me. Number one, God had given me what He wanted to—we were done with the woo-woo meditations. I had my orders. It was time to move. Number two, the battle of light and dark was both representative of the space I was physically in, which was not aligned with who He is, and of the battle against the unseen that lies in the path of all who are called to love Jesus and be His hands and feet in the world. (Of which we need not be afraid, by the way.)

I had great clarity, yet I had just wrapped up "fear day" and still had this sense of not-enoughness. I couldn't understand why. Maybe the meditation didn't work because I was stuck? Cue the tears. I had traveled all this way, and it seemed at that moment like it was for nothing. God had given me clarity on purpose and shown me that fear wasn't my portion, but I still felt that heavy sense of "I'm not enough." Maybe I wasn't enough to be enough. It's almost comical in hindsight. But at that moment, it felt like God was asking for the impossible, for me to be love while still fighting my own not-enoughness battle. I felt crushed.

I took a walk with a friend who I'd met there and had quickly become an anchor for me. Someone who got me and appreciated me for who I was. I told him how the meditation didn't work and asked, "What do I need to do to get rid of this not-enough thing?" He asked if I trusted him. "Sure, why?" He told me to close my eyes and close my mouth and not open them for any reason. "Uh, ok..." And then he plugged my nose, just long enough for it to be uncomfortable. He let go and said, "There's your permission. You're alive, so you have permission to live."

At that moment, I realized enoughness isn't something I embody, but it's a choice. I had to give myself permission to choose enoughness. Not-enoughness wasn't something that I could magically let go of, but enoughness was something I could actively choose. It finally sunk in— because I was alive, I was enough. My existence is the baseline for my enoughness. Nothing about me had to change. Only my perception and my way of thinking needed to change. God hadn't failed me. The process hadn't failed me. The process was just part of His process in getting me to this awareness. All I needed to do was change the story. To change how I think about enoughness. And that's true for you too. That's what is beautiful about this. Nothing about you except your perception needs to change.

Here's the deal, enoughness is a choice that you make moment to moment. Day-to-day. It's a continual choice. It's a commitment to yourself. And it's an opening to God. 2 Thessalonians 1:11 (NIV) always stops me in my tracks. "So we constantly pray for you, that our God may make you worthy of His calling." That He may make you worthy. He does that, and all we have to do is show up and be available to it. He says, "Come home, child. Claim the power, purpose, and peace that has always been yours. Take the courage that is available to you." Take courage. Not manufacture courage, but TAKE IT. He's standing with open arms to wrap you in peace and open hands to give you the courage you need. But you need to choose. Over and over and over again. And in time, it will get easier, more default. Over time you'll see the proof of His grace, His protection, and His provision.

PART THREE: YOU'RE NOT ALONE

*"While we are all lacking in ways, all broken in areas,
we are still loved and seen as whole and perfect
in the eyes of our Father."*

This continual choosing is an interesting new space, and there is a lot of room for shame to show up in this space. Not-enoughness loves shame. It leverages shame to keep you small. We'll talk about ego in Chapter 5 in a lot more detail, but know, for now, there is a part of you on the subconscious level that is deeply committed to this story that you're not enough, and to the illusion that is enoughness. That means there is an opportunity for you to have grace with yourself. Because you didn't consciously choose this, it's wired and trained into you from childhood.

And you need to hear this. You are not alone. I know we've talked a little about how not-enoughness impacts everyone with a heartbeat, but you need to really hear this. It's not just you. You're not broken. You're not the only one that struggles with enoughness. Some people hide it masterfully, but that's all it is. It's a mask. Even the people who have done the work and gone on their growth journey of returning to their powerful and authentic selves will have not-enough thoughts. They just have a skill set to handle it or bounce back faster from those thoughts.

I learned one of my favorite tools for the bounce-back from Dr. Kristin Neff, a researcher on self-compassion and mindfulness. Self-compassion is crucial here because it's the opposite in so many ways to the shame cycle we put ourselves through with our stories that we aren't enough. There are three pillars of self-compassion, as she explains it. Self-kindness, common humanity, and mindfulness. She describes self-kindness as being "gentle and understanding with ourselves rather than harshly critical and judgemental." Common humanity means "feeling connected with others in our experience of life, rather than feeling isolated and alienated by our suffering." And mindfulness is where we "hold our experience in balanced awareness, rather than ignoring our pain or exaggerating it." [4]

In a webinar with Dr. Neff, she taught a self-compassion break based on the three pillars of self-compassion. The first stage, self-kindness, is all about naming and acknowledging what you're feeling—really getting curious about it. The second stage, common humanity, is focused on how we are not the only one who has struggled with the emotions we just named, that they are part of the human experience. And the third stage, mindfulness, is about being with ourselves without trying to fix things. About reminding ourselves, "Hey, I'm here, and we've got this," and then sitting with the emotion while it dissipates, breathing into it, being still.

We talk about this here because the common humanity part of this is vital when we are exploring the reality that we aren't the only ones who struggle with enoughness and all the emotions that accompany that struggle. When we attach ourselves to the story that it's only us, we further the belief that we aren't enough because we feel that no one else struggles with this, and thus we must be lacking, broken, and unworthy. That's complete and total ego-based crap. It's fundamentally untrue. While we are all lacking in ways, all broken in areas, we are still loved and seen as whole and perfect in the eyes of our Father.

There is something so powerful about knowing you're not alone in the struggle. That other people get you and get what you're going through. It's healing. It helps conquer shame. I was chatting with a friend who experienced significant childhood trauma, and one of the biggest challenges for him was that he thought he was the only one. He thought no one else understood. No one else was as broken as he was. And then he met some incredible humans that were doing their own recovery work, and it was as if he was seen for the first time. It opened something up in him. It was a launching ground for him to be able to do more healing and more coming back to himself. Because he could see himself differently, as part of a larger community instead of alone on the journey and fundamentally different, he could let go of some of the shame and judgement he'd carried with him and lean into healing.

This is available for you when you start to see that it's not just you. You will look at yourself differently. You can begin to unravel some of the narratives and stories you've built around yourself and instead identify with who you actually are. And that opens space to come back to yourself. Space to embrace that, just maybe, you are enough. However, the question remains—Are you willing to choose it?

CHAPTER FOUR

TOO MUCHNESS

PART ONE: TOO MUCH

"Hiding behind too muchness is a way for us to get out in front of potential rejection and failure."

Choosing to see yourself as enough is one thing, but we also need to contend with this–Have you ever felt like you're too much? Have you been told that you're too loud? Too emotional. Too bossy. Too serious. Too big. Too bold. Too much of a dreamer. Have you been told that you want too much? Or that your dreams are too large? Have you had a moment when you wanted to speak up, but you chose not to? When you wanted to dance and be silly, but you chose to be quiet?

When I think about too-muchness, I used to think it was in opposition to not-enoughness. Now I see that it's intricately interconnected. Our too-much stories feed into our not-enough stories. Our not-enough stories underpin our too-much stories. Being too much can always be reframed as not enough of something else. Too loud becomes not quiet enough. Too bossy becomes not demure enough. Too serious becomes not fun-loving enough.

My too-muchness has always been very closely tied to "don't let your head get too big." I held the idea that the worst thing possible is to be egotistical. And that dreaming big equaled egotistical. Thinking you know things equates to being egotistical. That wanting too much is selfish. That being too loud is obnoxious. For years, my laugh-it-off phrase was, "I'm loud and obnoxious sometimes."

Too muchness gets defined in a lot of ways. Much like with not-enoughness, I can say with certainty that if you give it a try, you can come up with a list that's longer than you anticipated of ways that you're too much. Go ahead. I'll wait.

When we buy into this too-much story and the expectations we perceive society to have about who we are supposed to be, we slip into playing small. We drift off the path that God's been diligently straightening for us, and we throw some curves, speedbumps, and roadblocks up. We take an offramp onto a completely different route. And then we wonder why things aren't working out.

Hiding behind too muchness is a way for us to get out in front of potential rejection and failure. Take a breath and feel your way into this. See how it lands. "If I don't dream too big, I can't fall as far. Then I have less to lose. Then I won't be judged by my family or my community. It's safer to keep things small and to dim my light."

Understand this, too muchness is a projection of other people's playing small stories onto you. A projection of their failures, fears, and attachment to society's expectations about who they are supposed to be. It's not about you. So stop making it mean something about you.

As much as I'm preaching here, this is true for me too. I have my too-much stories that I'm still working on. For example, I have always wanted to perform on stage. There has been something in my soul my whole life that wanted to be a singer. That wanted to be out in front of people. It calls to me. But I dismissed it. I buried it. I justified my way out of it through both my not enough and too-much stories. I chalked it up to, "Nope, that's egotistical." And, "You can't be rich and a good Christian." And, "Musicians don't make enough money." And, "What if people don't think you're good enough? What if I get judged? What if I fail?" See the tie to not-enoughness?

This is a GOD-GIVEN GIFT that I possess. It's a skill that I have. It's natural for me. I've been told that my voice is healing. That it's powerful. And I BURIED IT! Song writing and music brought me through the toughest years of my life—when I was a moody and insecure teenager experiencing two years of intense bullying and the impacts on my self-esteem that came with it, writing songs was the one way I could process my emotions. It's how I came back to who I was. It was a way for me to be authentic when I felt there weren't other places to be me. And it's how I connect to God.

But I buried that gift because I was convinced that it was too big and too bold and too risky and that I'd be too much. I found little ways to express it, like singing at church and voice lessons, but it was always a playing-it-safe and staying small way of handling things. Not a full jump into what He called me to. I wasn't listening. I would continually tune out that inner voice that nudged me towards singing, and then I'd run my stories on repeat about how I was not talented enough, how people would judge me, and how it was egotistical to want to be on stage.

At the same time, I was battling a story that I talk too much and I'm too bossy. I've always been a talker. I know that I process verbally. And I'm someone who takes charge. Someone who leads and organizes, and sparks both people and change. I labeled these traits as "loud and obnoxious" and tried to bury them too. Again, I'd find small and "safe" ways to try to be authentically me. Leading committees, saying yes to volunteer support positions, and then essentially taking over. Even running my business was a space where I could find an outlet, but it still wasn't fully me. It was me metered down to be more acceptable. It was me avoiding rejection.

It's funny looking at it from the other side of this growth journey I'm on because all this desire for the stage, the speaking, the leading, the sparking people, the writing is what God is calling me to. Everything that I've been avoiding, everything that I have labeled as too-much, is EXACTLY WHAT GOD PUT IN ME TO DO THE WORK HE HAS CALLED ME TO!

Here's what's cool about God—He creates paths for us. PLURAL. He knows we are going to falter. And then He gives us opportunities and on-ramps back to what He calls us to. He has more than one path that He can make straight. But you must understand that by hiding behind this too muchness nonsense, you are throwing roadblocks into God's plan for your life. You are getting in the way instead of being on your way. Stop it. The cost is too great.

Here's the reality of you stepping off the path. Number one: Following equals fulfillment. When you take your own road and jump onto a different path, you're leading yourself straight to burnout, overwhelm, and a life that you know could have been more than it is. Number two: There are people placed along the path He has made straight for you that you are meant to serve, shake up, love, or create impact with that WILL NOT GET YOU because YOU WILL NOT PASS BY THEM. The people God has strategically placed along your path, that He has intended for you to be His hands and feet with, won't see the impact or transformation through you that He wants for them because you got caught up hiding behind too muchness. Are you willing to live a life that doesn't ultimately equate to impact and fulfillment? Are you willing to detour past the people you're assigned to?

There is this story in Ezekiel 47 about a river flowing from a temple. There is a lot of symbolism in this story. For example, God is the source of life, and staying connected to Him means living an abundant life. But, when I think about the cost of hiding behind too muchness, what strikes me is that this man in the story is led up along the river, crossing it a few times, each time finding the river is getting deeper, and then when it becomes too deep to swim he and his guide turn and look back along the riverbank (aka. the path) along which they traveled.

The text says, "I was surprised by the sight of many trees growing on both sides of the river" (Ezekiel 47:7). A little further on, it gives more context on these trees, "Fruit trees of all kinds will grow along both sides of the river. The leaves of these trees will never turn brown and fall, and there will always be fruit on their branches" (Ezekiel 47:12). To me, the trees are people, and the river is your path. When you walk in and embrace all the too-muchness that has been intentionally placed in you, when you trust Him along the way, people along your path will be impacted and grow; they will be fruitful and find healing, and they will live abundantly. That is, as long as you walk your path. That sounds like fulfillment and impact to me.

PART TWO: YOU'RE NOT HERE TO FIT IN

"Belonging is authenticity. Fitting in is forcing yourself into a box."

Our desire to fit in drives our need to avoid being too much. While writing this book, I put myself into a boot camp for authors. And for the first week, I played right into this narrative. I intended to show up strong. Show up as Coach Juli. Show up and be authentic and powerful. But entering this group of incredible women (none of whom I knew), putting myself into a new arena, pouring energy into this process, and feeling a little underwater meant that I defaulted into some old patterns. Through my perceptions and way of thinking, I started to gauge how I was perceived. I moved right into perception management mode, and before I knew it, I wasn't raising my hand when I wanted to. I wasn't speaking up when I wanted to. I wasn't asking questions or sharing experiences when I felt called to because I was worried about fitting in.

This is a back-up-the-truck realization moment. When we can catch it, we can choose to pause and observe what's happening. Jesus was very clear, we're not here to fit in. But we desire to fit in, don't we? Just like little Juli wanted to be popular and liked so that I would be enough, grown-up Juli still wants to be liked, admired, and affirmed. But ultimately, it's about belonging, not fitting in.

Brené Brown does a beautiful job of defining belonging:

"[Belonging is] the innate human desire to be part of something larger than us. Because this yearning is so primal, we often try to acquire it by fitting in and seeking approval, which are not only hollow substitutes for belonging, but often barriers to it. Because

true belonging only happens when we present our authentic, imperfect selves to the world, our sense of belonging can never be greater than our level of self-acceptance." [5]

Belonging is authenticity. Fitting in is forcing yourself into a box. Belonging is falling into God's arms and knowing He doesn't need you to change who you are. Fitting in is buying into someone else's story for your life.

When we play small and avoid being too much (too powerful, too loud, too bright, too successful, or whatever else hits your list), we are trying to bury part of ourselves, and that's where the lack of belonging originates. Not only that, but as we bury our talents or dreams or characteristics, they leak out in spurts anyway. It's just not always in a way that is intentional or even helpful. What we give energy to grows. What we try to push down builds up pressure and creates an uncontrolled explosion. What we get to do instead is to own our too-much traits and stories – so they don't own us. So they don't create the exact results we were trying to avoid in the first place.

Let's use my loud and obnoxious story as an example. I remember sitting in a church executive team meeting after deciding that I was usually too bossy and too opinionated. I knew that combination typically ended with me owning more of the follow-up tasks, responsibility, or emotional baggage than I should have. I walked in intending to let other people do the talking, make the decisions, and create the momentum. I'd talk less. I'd save my thoughts and only share if I felt called and after everyone else had a chance to speak. I told myself over and over, "Shut up, Juli." There were two problems. First, I had trained the group to move with my dominant nature. I had been named as chair of our Executive Team at four months pregnant with my second child. I was expected to be a leader in the space. My quietness threw them. Second, I was practically jumping out of my seat because I had so much to say while trying to contain my energy so that I wouldn't be "too much" again. Eventually, I pretty much erupted. All my opinions, thoughts, and feelings came out in one massive wave and overwhelmed the entire meeting. I don't know about you, but that looks like legitimately too much to me. I'd tried my best to be calm but ended up bossy and overbearing. If I'd owned the traits instead and walked into the meeting being conscious of allowing others an opportunity to speak and being authentically and powerfully me, we would have had a much more productive meeting.

Sometimes, the impact of avoiding too muchness is less of a "leaking out" or "explosion" of a buried trait. When too-muchness is more of an outcome, we often avoid it through self-sabotage. One of my biggest fears (that I didn't even know I had for many years) was being too successful. And it was a real-life challenge for me as I built a thriving real estate business. Because I attached making money to greed, because I worried that people would judge me for not being worthy of the success I was achieving, because I was convinced that I wasn't enough to maintain more, I'd subconsciously sabotage myself. I'd lose a client opportunity at work that normally I would win because I was checking out subconsciously. I'd show up differently. I'd be lazy instead of my typical go-getter, box-checking, make-sure-it's-done-on-time self. I'd ensure that I wouldn't get too close to "successful" and thus avoid the risk of judgment or failure. And then the self-sabotage I'd just used to avoid "too successful" would trigger the "not-successful enough" stories again. It was a spiral.

Here's what I've learned. You're not here to be concerned with how society thinks you should be. You're here to be a light. To be a tree-shaker. To be a change-maker. To challenge the ways of the world and stand for something better. And if HE MAKES YOU WORTHY, then whoever He has made you to be is not too much. There is no lack and no overdoing. Your authentic and whole self is exactly what is needed in this season and this moment.

Maybe the people He is calling you toward need your goofiness to remind them that they can find joy in the small moments. Maybe they need your boldness to shake them awake. Maybe they need the researcher in you to pull together pieces and consolidate information in a new and empowering way. He created you as you, not as someone naturally quieter or louder, not as more introverted or extroverted, not as someone different from you. He created you as you. Full stop. You are wonderfully made, remember? Full of wonder. But you've got to stop being a roadblock to your own life and to His plan for your life. Instead, it's time to be a permission slip for others to be their authentic selves and to live their calling. What would that be like for you if your life was a permission slip for someone else's authenticity? What if you could help them understand that they belong to God and themselves, and that's enough?

PART THREE: RECLAIMING TOO MUCH

"The only way to reclaim your too-muchness is to understand that you created it."

Here's the flip side to worrying about being too much. You could embrace it. The goal is to stop burying parts of us. Remember that is a disconnect from who we are and a disconnect from belonging. The goal is to get clarity about who we are and about what is just a coping mechanism or self-protective strategy. We'll go into detail on that later, but for now, here's part of the problem with "I'm too much" labels. We take them on as identity statements. We make those definitions part of who we are. Except that it isn't who we are. It's not our essence. It's not who we were made to be. It's not how God sees us.

Let's remember that we are made in the image of our Creator. We have a God who literally created everything. He's a pretty big deal. He can be the epitome of loud and quiet. He is both extremes of bold and subtle. He is ultimately nurturing and also fierce. He's abundance personified, He's generous, and He is everything good and then some. Our God is the embodiment of too much! And you are made in His image. He is in you. You reflect Him. If that's true, can you reach into "be strong and courageous" a little differently (Joshua 1:9)? If you are created to be light, go out into the world and be love, and speak and act for Him, is it possible that it will require you to embrace what you have thought of as too much? To be too much?

Here's the opportunity. Let's reclaim "too much." Let's live our "too much" lives. Let's take the power back that we have given to all the societal expectations, family standards, and places and spaces where we have abandoned ourselves to fit in. Let's instead be authentically and wholly us.

Believe me, I get the tension that can show up here. Lately, I've been getting the message to "Be bold for me," which means being more overt about my faith. Inevitably the question "what if it's too much?" has run through my head about eight thousand times. I was raised in a church where we struggled to get people to clap their hands, so being bold about my faith feels more than a little foreign. In my ten years in real estate, I bought a story that you don't talk about religion or politics. It's uncomfortable to mentally explore. But then I remind myself who I am in Him, and I choose to show up anyway. I choose to stretch the edges of my comfort zone. Why? Because I know I'm called to speak on stage, write books, and create a massive impact. I know I'm powerful, capable, and smart. I know I'm goofy and loud. And I'm going to own it. All of it.

This part gets me fired up every time. When I look at playing small or hiding my light, accommodating others or avoiding conflict and rejection, and all the behaviors that showed up when I was avoiding my too-muchness, I realize that my way of DOING led to my way of BEING. And this is true for you too. Your way of doing has led to your way of being. That is a self-responsibility moment because the only way to reclaim your too-muchness is to understand that YOU CREATED IT. YOU HAVE ALLOWED THESE STORIES TO PERSIST. And that is AMAZING! It means that you have the POWER to choose to do differently and hence, BE differently. And you don't have to figure that out on your own. One of my favorite passages in the Bible about this is Romans 12:2. It says, "Don't copy the behavior and customs of this world, but let God transform you into a new person by changing the way you think. Then you will learn to know God's will for you which is good and pleasing and perfect."

Let God transform you and change the way you think. Allow God in. This is key because if we attempt this journey of reclaiming too much without Him, if we don't ask Him for clarity about who we are, if we aren't working to be more like Him, we can get pulled off into yet another story about who we should and shouldn't be. And the avoiding of your too-muchness will inevitably resume. What's also important about this verse is the word then. First, you transform. First, you let Him transform you. And then, you will get clarity on what your path is and what you're here for. "Then you will learn to know God's will for you, which is GOOD, and PLEASING, and PERFECT." When we allow Him to transform us and change how we think, then our purpose can and will come. It requires us to let go of old thought patterns, baggage, and stories. It requires us to instead lean into faith.

It's time to be you. It's time to be authentic. Your power lies in your authenticity. His power flows through in your authenticity. **BE. TOO. MUCH.**

Hear me. YOU BELONG. All of you. The too much and the not enough and everything in between. All your fire. All your calm. All your loud. All your quiet. All your love. All your anger. All your knowing. All your questioning. All your compassion. All your selfishness.

You belong. You belong to you. You belong to a loving God. Stop trying to be someone else. Be you. Be who He created you to be.

CHAPTER FIVE

MEET YOUR EGO

PART ONE: YOUR EGO AND ITS JOB

"Your ego will do everything it can to maintain the status quo because the ego is the keeper of the status quo."

Do you know what keeps you in your not-enoughness? What keeps you avoiding too muchness? What keeps fear in play? It's called your ego, and I like to think of it as a subconscious four-year-old that throws tantrums to get its way. I grew up understanding the word ego in terms of egotistical. It tied right into those "too muchness" stories we just looked at, and it was something to be avoided. That's not what we are talking about here. Let's take a minute and get clear on the concept of your ego.

We're talking about the part of your personality defined by the Encyclopedia Britannica this way:

"[The ego] which is experienced as the "self" or "I" and is in contact with the external world through perception... comprises the executive functions of personality by serving as the integrator of the outer and inner worlds... The ego gives continuity and consistency to behavior by providing a personal point of reference which relates the events of the past (retained in memory) with actions of the present and of the future (represented in anticipation and imagination)." [6]

Let's run that back in plain English. Your ego forms your sense of self and informs how you perceive and interact with the world. It wants the certainty and definitiveness that exist when you behave consistently. It wants control. It tries to understand where you are and uses that frame of reference to predict where you're going. I heard Dr. Kristin Neff refer to it essentially this way in a workshop in early 2020. It's part of you that has one primary job, to keep you safe. And she said to do that, your ego wants three things: certainty, definitiveness, and control.

Your ego questions and makes assumptions about whether what you're about to do is safe or not and if you can get your needs met there. Our ego (sense of self) comes into play when we're young because our sympathetic nervous system and amygdala (part of your brain) both have the job of instigating fear responses [7] to keep us safe. The ego takes those messages from our inner world and translates them into how we need to behave to survive in our outer world. Put differently, the ego functions as the voice of those systems.

Hence, when your ego makes decisions and assumptions about what is safe, it's evaluating through an existing frame of reference. From a perspective of "I understand where we are now. And I understand where we've been. But I don't understand what could be on the other side of the growth, the shift, or the change that we will experience if we change how we behave, how we show up in a relationship, or who we think we are..." Whether you're implementing new habits or developing a new mindset, your ego shows up evaluating that change if you shift anything in your life to something new.

Your ego doesn't want change. If you're at point A and want to go to point B, but point B is new, the possibilities of danger are endless. A bear could jump out from behind the next minivan. Thankfully, our brains are complex, and we have the capacity to redirect our ego and make choices to move anyway–thanks, frontal lobe! [8]

Consciously, because you have life experience and context on the world, you know that a bear jumping out at you is not reality. You have an idea of what's possible if you move toward point B. Your ego, though? It knows you haven't been there before. So, by default, it must not be safe. This means your ego doesn't want to allow you to make a move in that direction. And then your ego leverages what we call self-protective patterns to keep you exactly where you are.

Here are some examples of those patterns:

- Imposter syndrome
- Comparison
- Perfectionism
- Overwhelm
- Denial
- Self-judgment
- Avoidance
- Procrastination

The list goes on, but you need to understand that your ego knows how to stop you. It knows what has stopped you before. It knows what has kept you in sameness. It knows what has worked to keep you safe. It will do everything it can to maintain the status quo because the ego is the keeper of the status quo.

And that's frustrating because consciously, you see yourself suffering, struggling, and dreaming of more but staying stuck. Consciously, you hear the whispers from God telling you that there is more in store for you, or you feel the pull of your heart to something else. But ego says, "It's okay. We're alive. We're surviving. And if you change or grow, that requires you to change how you think, which will then change how you show up. And there's no definitiveness there. Let's not do that."

Your ego can't control the outcomes. It can't be certain of what things will look like. It can't be certain about your safety or if you can get your needs met on the other side of change. This brings us right back to fear, and the power fear has in underlying ALL of the patterns and behaviors that keep you small.

Because your ego doesn't have a frame of reference for new or different or what's on the other side of change, it will tell you that you don't want the change. It will ask you questions like who do you think you are? Why would you even bother? What would people think? It's going to make you as uncomfortable as possible. It's going to throw up some overwhelm. It's going to say, "Look at what you don't know." Or, "Look how many other people are already doing this." Your ego's target is to create so much fear that you won't move. It triggers shame and tries to convince you that you are not enough. And then your ego has done its job because you're "safe" and you're the same.

Let's circle back though for a minute to this: "Let God transform you into a new person, by changing the way you THINK" (Romans 12:2). Stepping through the fear and the overwhelm, trusting a God who has always been good, who makes all things work together for your good, means knowing that He provides us the space to change how we think and to go to battle with our ego. This verse, which is prefaced by "Don't copy the behavior and customs of this world," is a permission slip to let go of comparison. It's a permission slip to let go of other people's standards for enoughness and what too much looks like.

PART TWO: SELF-PROTECTIVE PATTERNS

"Self-protective patterns keep you safe in your subconscious context, but they keep you small in your reality."

Changing the way we think requires us to identify, and start to detach from, self-protective patterns. At its most basic, a self-protective pattern is a behavior that we use to keep ourselves safe or get our needs met. Because we aren't capable of loving perfectly or receiving love perfectly, we learn when we are young what behaviors work to get our needs met and what works to keep us safe. And then, we repeat those behaviors until they turn into a pattern—a reaction and response that is habitual and primarily subconscious. We wrap those patterns around ourselves as part of our personality development, and they inform how we interact with and perceive the world. They become a lens we look through. This means that personality, in essence, is a collection of self-protective patterns. Dr. Beatrice Chestnut refers to personality as "a part of your character that develops to interface with the outside world." [9] Ian Morgan Cron and Suzanne Stabile, in their book, The Road Back to You, explain it this way:

> *"As little kids, we instinctually place a mask called personality over parts of our authentic self to protect us from harm and make our way in the world. Made up of innate qualities, coping strategies, conditioned reflexes, and defense mechanisms, among lots of other things, our personality helps us know and do what we sense is required to please our parents, to fit in, to satisfy the expectations of our culture, and get our basic needs met." [10]*

What's key here is these patterns start out serving us. They have a purpose, and they are actually helpful, to a point. Our ego leverages self-protective patterns as part of its responsibility to keep us safe. Good old ego, it's a behavior driver. The challenge is that as we get older, not only does our ego layer more and more of these self-protective patterns around us and around the essence of who we are, but they get more automatic, and we begin to believe that our patterns are our identity

Another thing happens as we get older. We outgrow the patterns. Essentially, we don't need them all the time because now we have context about the world. We have life experiences. We have a fully developed pre-frontal cortex. But we have been operating in the way we are currently operating for so long and thinking through the same lens for so long that it's a default. It's all we know, and our ego is downright attached to our current way of being. This means we have self-discovery work to do, and from there, we can begin to actively detach from these patterns that are running us.

One of the most prominent self-protective patterns I have learned to disentangle myself from is people-pleasing. When I think about being that awkward, try-hard kid, I see it showing up there. I said yes to playing the games that my friends wanted to play. I waited to see what movie other people wanted to watch before I spoke so that I could adjust my response to what I thought would help me fit in. I had crushes on the same celebrities that my friends did. I played teacher's pet.

As I got older, I became more and more entrenched in this pattern, not wanting to ever hurt someone's feelings. Carrying the responsibility of how everyone around me was feeling. Avoiding conflict. Saying yes when I wanted to say no. Overcommitting myself continually. I brought it with me everywhere I went. It meant that

I had very few boundaries, and I didn't know how to take care of myself first. As far as I was concerned, taking care of me first (or pretty much at all) was not acceptable. Everyone else first, then me. But I was never done with everyone else.

I brought people-pleasing into my marriage, trying to guess what my husband would want so that he would be happy. I brought it into visits with family, attempting to be the version of me that would make them the proudest and most comfortable. I brought it into my business, continually going over and above for people to the detriment of myself. I brought it into parenting, volunteering, charitable giving, and friendships. It was everywhere.

That's the thing with self-protective patterns. They don't just show up in one place. They show up everywhere because we are one person, and we see life through our lens, which is filtered by our personality. It wasn't until I completely hit the wall and burnt myself out that I started to see how this was destructive. I didn't think I was worthy of putting myself first. I thought it was selfish. And I thought it was normal. As it turns out, not everyone struggles with people-pleasing and boundaries in the way I did.

Some people struggle with denial because if they admit that something is wrong, that means they failed. Some people struggle with conflict because they believe that they can't be happy unless everyone around them is happy. Others struggle with fear and believe they need a contingency plan for every possible outcome. All of us have multiple patterns. And all of us get to decide if we are going to let those patterns, and our ego that drives them, control our lives.

Here's the truth, they're patterns. They're stories. Self-protective patterns keep you safe in your subconscious context, but they keep you small in your reality. If you let the ego drive, you give it your power. That's not God's plan for you.

CHAPTER SIX

THE EGO BATTLE

PART ONE: MEET YOUR CRITIC

"Fear underpins your self-protective patterns, and it drives your ego."

Now that we have a sense of the ego, its job, and what it's using to keep you safe, it's time to meet Bertha. Okay, it's actually time to meet that inner critic who lives in your head and acts as the ego's voice, but mine happens to be named Bertha.

One of the most powerful ways our ego keeps us safe and playing small (which ultimately equates to us remaining unchanged) is through language. And the voice of the ego is that critical inner voice that says things like, "I'm so stupid." "What was I thinking?" "They must think I'm crazy." Or, "Why even bother trying? I always fail." This voice is judgemental, and it speaks to and confirms all our not enough stories.

In his book, Positive Intelligence, Shirzad Chamine talks about the Inner Critic as the Judge. A universal saboteur as something that gets in our way, sabotages our intentions, and steals our power. It has a predisposition to exaggerate the negative and assume the worst. It's hardwired into us as a survival mechanism. He says that it helps us create a mental construct through which we can perceive the world and our life experiences. [11]

But so often, that mental construct, or lens and frame of reference, is not helpful, and it keeps us stuck. And that takes us right back to changing the way we think and allowing God to transform us. We need a new mental construct, a new frame of reference, a new lens of who we are. Of our enoughness, purpose, and personal power.

Remember, when we sit in our not-enoughness and choose that not-enough mindset, we contradict God, who says we can do ALL things through Christ who gives us strength (Philippians 4:13). ALL things. Not some things. Not only safe things. All things.

Let's get tangible here. Under the desire for safety that our ego so desperately chases is fear. Fear is driving you and your life. And you've given fear your power. It's time to take it back.

As we have been talking about, fear underpins your self-protective patterns, and it drives your ego. Bertha has shown up so many times while I've been working on this book, telling me that I don't know what to say, asking why anyone would want to listen to me. Why do I think I belong on bookshelves taking up space when Brené Brown or Mel Robbins could be there instead? It's the same kind of negative self-talk that had me playing small for years and sabotaging myself. The "I can't." The "I don't know how." The "what if they judge me?"

But Bertha is often wrong. She used to tell me I'm not business-minded enough. That I don't know what I'm doing running a business. That I'm not entrepreneurial. And then I built a half-a-million-dollar-a-year company. Or there were times Bertha said my voice wasn't good enough and no one would want to listen to me sing. But then I would sing at church and get feedback about how powerful and healing my voice is. Wrong again, Bertha. Oh, and don't forget the mom-shaming talk. Bertha showed up again, telling me that I'm completely ruining my kids and I suck as a mom. All the while being affirmed by friends, my husband, my kids themselves, and our family psychologist that I'm doing a great job with them and that they're lucky to have me.

So when I started to write this book and Bertha showed up saying I don't know how to write a book, and I will fail, and I can't, and I shouldn't, when she asked what will people think, and am I a strong enough Christian, do you know what I told her? Thanks, Bertha, but I got this.

Do you know why I've got this? Because my God has me. And HE SAYS that I can do ALL things through Him. He says that I am his daughter. He says that He gives me everything I need. And He says to go do this thing. Seriously, it's not even my book. He's just using my hands.

Suck it, Bertha.

Quick side note. Some people have a whole committee of voices, and some have just one. Name them. Being able to refer to my inner critic as Bertha allows me to distance grown-up conscious me from ego me. It allows me to zoom out on the words and the voice and get curious about it. It gives the voice a more tangible identity so I can call it out. "Hey, Bertha. Thanks, but I got this."

PART TWO: HUGS NOT PUNCHES

"We can appreciate our ego for how it always shows up for us to try to protect us and help us find ways to be okay."

It's time to talk about the ego battle. When we think of a battle, we think of a fight. Maybe it's a sword fight that comes to mind, or a yelling match. I think of boxing, particularly trading punches. And if you're thinking that going to battle with your ego means throwing punches, I'm here to tell you otherwise.

I know, I know, it would seem more fun that way, right? Throwing a knock-out punch to your ego? Putting it in its place? Towering over it and watching it slink away?

This battle, though, is hugs, not punches. Our ego is a part of us, not something separate, so beating it up is also beating ourselves up. This battle is won with compassion and curiosity rather than shaming ourselves. It's won with gratitude and grace instead of anger. Your ego is not something that you can, or should, get rid of. It has a purpose, and going to battle is about the stories you tell yourself.

When we try to bury our ego, much like when we try to bury our too-muchness, it gives it more power because we have to use so much energy to hold it off. Have you ever tried to hold a soda bottle lid on after shaking it up? Eventually, pressure builds up enough for the liquid to leak out the cracks or blow the lid off. That's essentially what happens with our ego when we try to pretend it doesn't exist. That leaking or blow-out may look like physical pain or injury. I've seen it show up in people close to me as shingles or auto-immune diseases. That leaking or blow-out may show up as your mindset diving into a victim space where you think everything is happening to you instead of for you. That leaking or blow-out may damage your relationships, your work, your confidence, and most importantly, your relationship with God.

Here's what we want instead—integration. Because your ego is part of you, it's important to allow it to exist. Instead of winding up to punch each other in the face, we pull each other in for a hug. It means that you give your ego a snuggle and start having a conversation with it. Treat it like you would a 4-year-old. This means being kind and compassionate to yourself. That's easier when we come to terms with how our ego is necessary and has served us.

Our ego may cause frustration or overwhelm now, but we can appreciate how, in truth, it helped us to survive a difficult childhood. Or to manage a mismatch of how we wanted to be loved compared to how our parents knew how to love us. Or to feel safe when we lost someone we cared about. We can appreciate our ego for how it always shows up for us to try to protect us and help us find ways to be okay. And we can look at all the patterns that may not serve us now, at least most of the time, and get curious about where they've been of value so that we can appreciate them too.

Let's get personal. My people-pleasing pattern helped me to get my needs for love met in a way that I could receive love. Perfectionism has allowed me to develop a skill set that has served both me and my clients as I've seen how things can be done better. My achiever nature is what God uses to move me boldly and quickly to where He needs me. My protective defaults that came out after being bullied as a teen has led to a passion for being a voice for the abused and the oppressed. It's not always easy to see how something served you or could have built you, especially when the things you may have faced are traumatic, and when there is no excuse for them or reconciling them. There may be things in your past that break God's heart and that He never wanted for you, but He is the Redeemer. Let this be the encouragement that although you may need to search for the gift in the patterns taking you out or getting in your way, the gift is always there. Because we serve a God who loves us and makes all things work together for our good and His glory. Even the crappy stuff.

Back to the "hugs, not punches," because we need to get tactical on the ego battle. The opportunity here is to bring ego in and get curious when it starts to throw a fit. We can ask this—what is it trying to keep us safe from? What lesson does it have for us? And then we can thank it for showing up in its 4-year-old context of the world to try to keep us safe. This is so key that it bears repeating. Your ego is a part of you that is trying to keep you safe. That's something to have gratitude for. And then, like with a child, we can remind it that we are ok. We've got this, and our Father God, He has us. Regardless of the storm we may be in, we are safe in His arms, in the center of the storm.

Essentially, we need to approach our ego with grace. Not our own grace, but a grace that comes with knowing and having a relationship with the Father. When we approach ourselves with love, we can approach this part of ourselves with that same love. And with compassion in knowing that our fear-driven ego no longer needs to hold so much control and power. Bringing it in, operating from curiosity, and being compassionate with ourselves puts us back in the driver's seat.

PART THREE: PATTERN INTERRUPTS

"We will not give our power to stories, fear, the enemy, or anything that may take us away from becoming who we are called to be."

When you decide to get in the driver's seat of your own life, you're throwing your ego into the backseat. It can hang out because it's a necessary part of you–you don't want to run off into life without a self-protective sense or instinct. Your ego and self-protective patterns still have a role to play, and it's more dangerous to try to drop them off on the side of the road. All that said, while I advocate bringing our ego in for a hug and a gratitude chat, sometimes we need a good firm word to remind it that we are the grown-up, and we are driving. How do we do that? Welcome to the pattern interrupt.

Over the years, I've gone back to a comedy clip over and over again with Bob Newhart playing a psychologist. A patient comes into his office, asks for his advice, general hilarity ensues, and his advice to her that is supposed to fix everything is two words–STOP IT! [12]

While this isn't how I'd advise you to deal with all your problems (hello bypassing and avoidance), it is powerful to speak over ourselves. The Word is a recurring theme in our faith as Jesus followers. Whether we are talking about the words that were spoken, and then creation followed, or the Word becoming flesh when Jesus came to live among us, or wisdom coming to us from being in the Word, words are powerful. One of the ways we refer to God is The Word. John 1:14 says, "So the Word became human and made His home among us." When we speak, we create our reality. We shift our perception. We tell our subconscious what to pay attention to.

"Stop it!" is a cue to our subconscious and our ego that we are not going to give our power to stories, fear, the enemy, or anything that may take us away from becoming who we are called to be. It's a way for us to interrupt our automatic reactions, not to mention our defaulting to our old patterns. Hence the name "pattern interrupt." We interrupt our existing pattern when we take a minute to breathe, step out of the story or the emotion that is showing up, and see things from the perspective of an observer.

I'll give you a real-life example. Whenever someone sends me a note that starts with "I want to talk with you..." my whole nervous system goes into story-making mode and assumes that something is wrong (hello, therapy!). Not only that, but I question and assess whether I may have done something wrong or have been perceived as doing something wrong. We're not even talking about situations where I have a tense relationship with someone. It could be a client who is a raving fan, full of integrity, and a sister in Jesus. My ego still goes into story mode. Old Juli would buy that story. Depending on when we were going to talk, I'd spend hours or days worrying and looking for ways that I was not enough. I'd try to get out in front of it. And then I would show up in that conversation expecting something bad. But ninety-nine percent of the time, it wouldn't be anything bad, and none of my story-making would prove to be true.

As I've grown and become more self-aware, I can usually see the story-making happening because I know it's one of my defaults. I know that I have a tendency, likely from being bullied as a teen, to expect the worst. I also know that I have a choice about going to that mental and emotional space. I'm no longer willing to give my power to unfounded stories. So I'll tell myself, "STOP IT!" And if that isn't enough, I'll add, "Not today, ego! We are NOT doing this today."

Watch the Bob Newhart skit. Seriously, it's the best. It brings humor into the pattern interrupt, which is important to shift your mindset and release hormones in your brain that function in opposition to the downward spiral you were about to experience.

When the ego persists and "Stop it! We are not doing this today" doesn't quite cut it, we can add physical movement to the process. Moving our body sends a cue to our subconscious about where to focus our energy and helps get us out of the thinking space where ego is often the strongest. My favorite way to bring the body in is to tap a table, chair, or surface next to me and say, "Have a seat over here. I've got this. God's got me. We're good. Ok, self? We're good." It's like evicting the ego from the driver's seat and specifying where its seat is. I am not getting rid of it but choosing to take my power back and be clear about my expectations for how I move forward. Essentially, this has the power to remind conscious us, grown-up us, that we are capable of stepping into our power and we are intentionally showing up. We get to choose what power we give to our ego and when to let it show up and serve us.

PART FOUR: FEELING THE FEELS

"You can experience both positive and negative emotions, not only at a thinking level but also as a physical sensation."

While we are in pattern interrupt and ego battle territory, we need to talk about feelings. Our culture has become so focused on achievement and what's next that we have forgotten how to be with ourselves, which is further complicated by forgetting who we are in the first place. When that happens, we start to bypass. This term used to confuse me, so let me define it simply for you: Avoiding, going around, and disconnecting us from how we feel.

This disconnection and avoidance rob us of the opportunity to come back to ourselves and be authentically and wholly us. Instead, when we do "our work," we step into a relationship with ourselves. And a healthy relationship with ourselves requires us to create space for our emotions.

So how do you even know what you're feeling? One of the most powerful exercises for me has been to pay attention to how feelings physically feel in my body. Here's what I have found fascinating about emotions manifesting physically—they show up in my body before my conscious mind can recognize and process them. It's true of all my psychosomatic body-feeling connections. They present physically first.

The first emotion I discovered was anxiety, which shows up as an upset stomach, almost a bubbly sensation, and a tight vibrating in my forehead. If it's really bad, I start burping. That may seem like too much information, but let's get transparent here. If you can be comfortable with my transparency, you can conquer being comfortable with your own. When that tension and vibration show up in my forehead and that unsettledness in my gut, I've learned "this is what anxiety feels like," meaning I can interrupt the pattern right there instead of letting it get stronger and take hold before I mentally catch on. It means I can slow and deepen my breathing and look for what the anxiety is telling me.

Shame was the next one I discovered. When I think about shame and experience shame, it starts as a lump in my throat and then extends up into my head and down into my heart as heaviness. Often, I will feel shame come up and have no idea why I feel it until I do some self-exploration. Take a minute and think through this one for yourself. See what you feel in yourself.

Fear is a more recent discovery. It presents as a tightness in my chest and shows up when I'm afraid or feel unsafe. It shows up with rejection. It shows up when I play small and know I am hiding. I describe it often as a contraction. That is fascinating because it's the opposite of how the Holy Spirit shows up. Fear is not of God. When I step into fear, I'm moving away from Him. But when He shows up, when I have something that He is giving me to share or do, I feel an expansiveness in my chest that almost can't be contained. This is so rewarding to me because as a natural feeler and emotional human, God uses my defaults to give me clarity. There is peace and excitement in that expansiveness. While He can show up, and I can hear Him in my mind at times, He also shows up in giving me "peace, which exceeds anything we can understand" (Philippians 4:7).

You can experience both positive and negative emotions, not only at a thinking level but also as a physical sensation. The more you can clue into them, the more you'll be able to clarify what you're feeling.

You might be thinking, "Ok, Juli, I have an emotion, but what am I supposed to do with it?" Well, don't bury it. Ok? Feel it. Got it? Good, we are done then. I'm kidding. First, recognize that emotions are temporary. They're data. They exist to tell us something. Anger, as an example, tells us that a boundary has been crossed or that we have a values misalignment with ourselves or others. Grief tells us that we have lost something that mattered to us. Fear tells us that there might be something unsafe happening. When we don't feel our feelings and allow ourselves to be with them, we rob ourselves of our power. It's like saying, "Hey self, you can't handle this emotionality coming. Let's avoid it."

Not only that, but also it means we aren't giving it to God. We aren't taking the opportunity to be in relationship with Him and ask Him what He wants us to learn through our experience. This is where spiritual bypassing comes in, going around God and trying to control everything on our own. But He uses ALL things to work together for our good (Romans 8:28), including our emotions. The opposite of bypassing is embracing and surrendering. Then we can ask ourselves, and ask God, what we have to learn or experience at this moment. What is it that He is building in us? What is He asking us to take off of ourselves or let go? What is it that created the circumstances for these feelings to exist in the first place? Is there something we need to evaluate when we get back to a place of emotional neutrality, where we aren't so emotionally sucked into the swirl that we can think straight? That's the target. Get to neutral first. To the place where you step back into your power so you can choose your response. And then we can start to move back into our power.

CHAPTER SEVEN

ESSENTIAL IDENTITY

PART ONE: WHO ARE YOU?

"We were all purposefully made—on purpose, with purpose, and for purpose."

We've given some serious time at this point in the journey of building a foundational understanding of what so often gets in the way of living our Fired-up, Fulfilled, and Free life. We've explored the not-enoughness and too-muchness that are so intertwined. We've developed an understanding of how fear and ego hold us captive. And we've looked at how to step through some of that tension. Now it's time for what was the most powerful and transformative piece of my journey. Getting clarity on the "Who am I?" question.

What is it that defines your identity beyond being His? The answer to that is different than what you might think. As a society, we drive home the message "you are what you do." "You are your roles." We act like they define us and our worth. And then we pass along that message to our kids, and the cycle continues. I ask this question of people all the time, and here are some of the answers I get:

- I'm a mom.
- I'm a business owner.
- I'm an entrepreneur.
- I'm a teacher.
- I'm an accountant.

- I'm a stay-at-home dad.
- I'm a volunteer.
- I'm a board member.
- I'm a wife.
- I'm a grandpa.

We tell ourselves that these roles and jobs are who we are. But they're not.

I get this at a very personal level. I used to define myself like this: "I'm Juli, a Boss, a realtor, an entrepreneur, a mom, a wife, a Christian, and a singer..." I measured myself against all of the expectations that I thought society had for my enoughness. Each of these areas had a checklist of everything I needed to do to be enough. I'm not kidding. I would physically create checklists, mind-mapping all the places where I had responsibility and everywhere that there was an expectation that I thought I needed to meet. And then I would get so overwhelmed by everything I needed to do and try to be, that I would self-sabotage. Or I'd completely avoid some areas so I could be exceptional in another.

When I was running my real estate business for ten years, I did it in proving mode. I was constantly chasing that hit of "Look, I proved I'm enough!" But those hits fade, so I'd be off looking for a chance to prove it again. Not to mention that I was giving up family time to do it. I was avoiding my faith to do it. I felt like I was failing in so many areas because, honestly, there was no way to measure up to this bar I had set for myself. I thought that being a successful businesswoman who made a lot of money and gave a lot away was the best way for me to be worthy of the life I had built. It was exhausting. I never actually felt worthy. There was always more to chase and more to reach for.

I finally hit a point where I was so burnt out that I couldn't fight anymore. More specifically, I couldn't do it without God anymore. He'd always been there, but I continually put roadblocks between me and Him. I didn't trust Him. I believed that I was somehow the one human who lived outside His grace. I was the one exception to the rule. I didn't realize how utterly ridiculous and egotistical that was until later. Maybe you get that, though. Maybe you're in a place where you believe it for other people but not for you. He'll show up for other people. He'll heal other people. He'll forgive other people. He'll provide for other people. But for me? No.

I had built this business on my own back, completely at the expense of myself and my identity. I was trying to make everyone happy. I was trying to manage all the details. Although I had a great team, I still carried all the responsibility and worry and was, in some respects, in go-it-alone mode.

And then I got asked the question, "Who are you without all of this? Who are you without your business, your family, your marriage, your volunteer commitments? What's left?" Do you know what I said? It's what most people say. "I don't know."

Hey there, ego!

Ask yourself those questions. See what comes up.

I sincerely didn't know. I was so attached to getting my worth from my work and meeting my needs through achievement that I could hardly separate myself from the doing and the proving. It wasn't just in my business and in real estate, though. It was that way since I was that try-too-hard little girl. Always trying to prove I was enough. What I hadn't learned yet was that I was using the wrong measuring stick.

After I got asked this "who are you without all of this?" question, I sat on the floor and listened to my worship list. I journaled. I cried. I asked God. "Who am I? Who am I, Lord? Please tell me what you see because all I see is me not measuring up. All I see is me so tired and empty that I don't know the answer." And then a word came to me. Love. You're love, Juli.

There was a whiteboard on the wall, and I wrote down love, and then this flow came—Love, joy, strength, light, grace. I stood back and looked at it, stunned. If I lost it all, everything, this was my essence. This was me at my core. This was who I am at my best. Who He created me to be. And then I realized that it was also Him. All these characteristics He placed in me reflected His characteristics and who He is. This was who I am and who I am in Him and who He is in me.

Mind blown.

But it didn't stop there. As I stood there, overjoyed and emotional, realizing there was more to me than my titles, I learned that we ALL are a collection of His characteristics, that we are all special snowflakes. I could be special and special to Him because He created me uniquely, just like a snowflake, and He also made you that way. I realized that we were all purposefully made—on purpose, with purpose, and for purpose.

I am love. I am joy. I am strength. I am light. I am grace. I am HIS. This was a breakthrough and one of the biggest ones of my life so far because now I could start to detach from placing my identity and worthiness in roles and assignments. I could instead learn to place it in who and whose I truly am.

PART TWO: THE FIRST LENS

"Knowing who we are lights a path back to ourselves."

Often when we think about identity, we tie it to our titles. We tie it to our successes and our failures. But we forget that who we are is above all of that. We live in expectation and obligation-filled boxes, surrounded by our perceptions of what other people think. We live caged in by limits that are placed on us by society and ultimately ourselves. We forget how powerful and capable our Father created us to be. That we were created to rule over the earth, and that's pretty powerful.

The concept of boxes has helped separate who I am from the roles I hold. Imagine a row of boxes on the ground, all lined up. And in big black marker on the side is mom, wife, real estate agent, entrepreneur, church elder, friend, house-maintainer, etc. Use your roles and places you give energy to—take a minute and make a list.

Each of those boxes has a defined checklist for enoughness (and usually one that isn't realistic). Now imagine swiping all those boxes to the side. Do you still exist? Of course, you do. Because your identity is not any of these things. They are areas in your life that you give your time and energy to. And who you are exists beyond any of these experiences and spaces. Who you are is an essence. It's spiritual. It extends beyond time. This essence shows up in us when we are our most authentic and powerful. It shows up when we are most aligned with our Creator God.

Fundamentally, this is the first lens that we leverage in a journey back to who God calls us to be. When you understand what you look like at your best and know who you are at an essence level, you can start to evaluate your current experience of life against it. Here are some questions that I had to work through after I got clarity on who I am:

1. Which areas do I continue to show up in at all?
2. What areas of my life that I'm currently in that don't align with me being my authentic self?
3. How much time and attention am I intentionally giving to each of these areas moving forward?
4. Which areas are the highest priority for me?
5. How does being love, joy, strength, light, and grace require me to show up in each area?

Your essence looks a bit like values. And there will always be some connection, if not complete overlap, between what you value and who you are. Clearly, right? Because who you are is foundational, and it determines what you value.

This lens of knowing who we are is also an incredible tool because it brings us back to neutral. On my journey, when I get triggered or sad, when I feel beat down, or when my ego is picking up the gloves to fight with me, I stop and say (out loud if I can) "I am love, I am joy, I am strength, I am light, and I am grace." It resets my nervous system. It reminds me of who I am. It brings me out of the patterns of pulling my value from others. It reminds me to filter this moment through the lens of who and whose I am, not the old lens of my self-protective patterning. It brings me out of fight or flight and back into power. It allows me to drop my walls so Jesus can show up. And then, I get to choose how to respond in a way most aligned with my identity and Creator.

I've also learned that tension shows up when there is a misalignment between who we are and how we behave or respond to life and its circumstances. Typically, something in my experience challenges my ability to show up as authentically me. Maybe I'm scared and operating from a place of fear, which is not congruent with "I am strength." Or I might be losing my temper with my kids, which is not in line with "I am love" or "I am grace." The misalignment exists outside of us too. And it's helpful to understand that it can be triggering when other people operate in contradiction to who we are. I may run into someone who has a real commitment to racist ideas. That's going to naturally trigger me because it doesn't line up with being grace or light or love. Likewise, I'll trigger myself if I actually overstep with the people I'm trying to support in my enthusiasm to be a good ally. I always go back to one of my favorite Andy Stanley quotes here – "Pay attention to the tension." [13] It exists to help you clue into your opportunities for improvement, places where you're out of integrity with yourself, and relationships and interactions that need some curiosity or maybe boundaries put into place. Paying attention, and developing honest awareness, may not be a fun process, but it's necessary for your growth and emotional and spiritual health.

Knowing who we are lights a path back to ourselves. Without it, we may try to grow and be better humans, but we're functioning directionless until we're clear on who we are and whose we are. When we don't know who we actually are and what we're here for, do you know what happens? We create boxes and give time and energy to things that aren't aligned with our values, purpose, or essence.

Knowing who we are at an essence level is also a giant permission slip for authenticity. And here's what's interesting about "I am" statements. Positive or negative, they get internalized subconsciously as part of who we are, which then drives our responses and our behaviors in life. That means who you tell yourself you are is FUNDAMENTALLY IMPORTANT. "I am" statements can empower and build us up or completely tear us down. They either reclaim our power or give it away, which impacts you in ways you don't even see. You have a choice here. A choice to see yourself as He sees you or at least work your way in that direction. Don't worry, you won't do it alone. Ask, and He will send you an army.

He calls you son or daughter. He calls you friend. He calls you beloved. And He is calling you deeper.

PART THREE: YOUR "I AM" STATEMENTS

*"Your Father God has placed
you here with purpose."*

Understanding who you are is crucial because it's the primary lens through which your life will be filtered from here on out. Buckle up. We're diving into clarity about your identity. But first, some context.

The exercise coming up is intended to help you break out of the boxes, not put you in one. You will build a shortlist of "I am" statements that represent you at your core and you at your best. They represent you at your most aligned with God. However, we are all infinite because we are made in the image of an infinite Creator. This is not an exercise about limiting who you are but rather focusing on a few key traits that make you uniquely you. It's about asking God, your Father, what He has placed in you that you can use as a reminder of who you are. That's the target.

We are creating an anchor. It's a set of words that bring you back to yourself. That will remind you who you are becoming. That will remind you of who He has made you to be. To guide you in becoming more like Him. It is context that you can use to create a roadmap back to yourself. As you work through this process, do what you need to do first to be in a receptive mindset. Ask God to show you who you are. Take a few deep breaths. And then grab a highlighter, a pen, and a notepad. Maybe turn on some meditative music. As you read through these, think of who you are, not who society tells you you're supposed to be. Think of you when you feel the most at home with yourself or the most in your power. Don't focus on you in your triggered or stressed-out states. Pay attention to the pull, strength, or feeling that shows up with each "I am." Highlight or circle anything that really lands with you, that feels right, or that you know is an important piece of who you are. Don't judge it, but instead, practice trusting the Holy Spirit to guide you.

First, a prayer:

Father God, guide us as we seek clarity from you about who you created us to be. Help us see through your eyes. Holy Spirit, be our guide. Help us drop all our expectations and stories about who we are supposed to be by society's standards to know who we are called to be by Yours. We seek You. We place our trust in You. In Jesus' name, we pray, amen.

Take a deep breath. Ready? Let's explore.

- I am bold.
- I am brave.
- I am resilience.
- I am compassion.
- I am contentment.
- I am creativity.
- I am discipline.
- I am love.
- I am diligence.
- I am enthusiasm.
- I am faith.
- I am courage.
- I am light.
- I am empathy.
- I am fire.
- I am calm.
- I am joy.

- I am determination.
- I am integrity.
- I am resourcefulness.
- I am wisdom.
- I am adventure.
- I am positivity.
- I am protector.
- I am optimism.
- I am grace.
- I am constancy.
- I am mercy.
- I am faithfulness.
- I am fierce.
- I am goodness.
- I am innocence.
- I am justice.
- I am intelligence.
- I am fun.
- I am independence.
- I am whole.
- I am visionary.
- I am humility.
- I am unique.
- I am honesty.
- I am perspective.
- I am gratitude.
- I am serenity.
- I am passion.
- I am momentum.
- I am confidence.

Is there anything else that is not on this list? Look at your shortlist. It may have four words. It may have fourteen. I've known some people to end up with half the list highlighted. There is no right or wrong here.

Now we get to narrow it down. Your target is to choose the three to six words that are the most powerful for you and that most wholly encompass who you are. To help you narrow it down, especially if you have half the list circled, go through the exercise again with the words that made your first-round shortlist and highlight the ones with it that feel particularly strong. From there, look for words that have similar meanings to you. Often you can narrow the list down by seeing how one word feeds into or encompasses another. You may look at your shortlist and know that some are less important and be able to drop them, or conversely, you'll find that you can easily pick out a few that land the most. You may hit resistance in the process and need to take time to come back to it. Ask God if He is telling you to take a break or if it's your ego showing up to throw some overwhelm into the equation.

Why three to six words? It's simple. It's so that you can remember them. This is important because you'll need to know them by heart to use them effectively. You'll need to be able to rattle them off daily, speak them when you hit resistance, and evaluate through them when you have a decision to make or come up against challenges on your journey.

Please remember that you are not saying you aren't the other words you highlighted. In fact, you hold all of the characteristics that resonated and more. To create an anchor that will ground you back to yourself, though, fifteen is just too many.

Once you get your shortlist, take the time to put them in order, and let Him guide you. There is a flow that often shows up. And what convinces me that He has a sense of humor is that when I sorted my words into Love, Joy, Strength, Light, and Grace, it just so happened to reflect the order of the fruits of the spirit, which I didn't connect the dots on for two and a half years. Talk about Him reminding me that I am a reflection of Him and made in His image. When you're done, add this. "I am His." This work isn't just who you are. It's whose you are too.

As you begin to use the "I am" statements, they'll feel like a pipe dream. You might catch yourself back in "If I embrace this, I'll be too much" or "I'm not good enough to claim that this is who I am." Welcome to the party, Ego! I might as well call you out right now before you even get there. Stop it! Your enoughness is settled, remember? It's an illusion. Your too-muchness is a societal perception. Avoiding being your authentic and powerful self flies in the face of who He created you to be. You get to choose who you are in every moment and know that it's not in your strength that you'll become more and more that version of you. It's in His grace, His plan, and His moving within and through you that creates that. Your job is to stop it with the roadblocks. Repeat after me. "He makes me worthy."

Know this too. There is a way to hack the resistance. I am becoming.

"I am becoming love."

"I am becoming joy."

"I am becoming strength."

"I am becoming light."

"I am becoming grace."

The becoming acknowledges that you are in process. So if you just can't get to a place of believability yet, give yourself the grace to be becoming.

One more thing, you may have noticed that I didn't put enough on the list of "I am's." We are all enough, and becoming enough is a choice. Do it if it resonates for you, and you're led to include it on your list. Let the Spirit lead—I won't get in His way on that one.

And remember this, "We are God's handiwork, created in Christ Jesus to do good works, which God has prepared in advance for us to do" (Ephesians 2:10, NIV). Your Father God has placed you here with purpose. He has created you for assignments and anointing that have been in play since before you were born. Know who you are, and then be ready to move when He says move.

PART FOUR: HELP ME SEE ME THE WAY YOU DO

"He shows up for us, but we must be active participants."

In the depths of my burnout, a transition had to happen for me to start to believe in this new sense of identity. I had my "I am" statements as my anchor, which was powerful in its own right. But I still saw all my flaws and my not-enoughness. I still compared myself continually to the people around me. But God, in all His foresight, sent me an army. He sent me people who saw past my walls, saw past my fear, and saw pieces of what was possible for me. These people started to call me up. They would speak over me about what they saw was possible. But part of me couldn't receive it. I was so committed to my old narrative and my not-enoughness that my body would physically recoil when something positive was said about me.

I had friends who said they would continue complimenting me and giving voice to my skills, talents, and nature until I got used to it and learned to receive it. I had to choose to be open. I had to choose to be available to see more in me than I had seen up to that point. And that was scary because it was unknown. It would require a change in how I think. And that meant I had an ego battle to fight between my current way of being and starting to see myself the way God does.

In that state of exhaustion and realizing something had to change, I stepped into the battle, surrounded by my army of friends, coaches, family, podcasts, audiobooks of mentors, and Jesus Himself on the front line. Over time, I realized that how people saw me was fundamentally different than how I saw myself. They saw me as more powerful than I saw myself. They saw me as more capable than I saw myself. They saw me as more generous than I saw myself. They looked to my future and saw me in places and spaces that I felt completely unworthy of and wanted to believe were unattainable but that were obvious fits for me in the eyes of my community.

This is the challenge with our frame of reference—we are zoomed in. We see through our current default lens, and it's limited. But when we are surrounded by people who can zoom out and stay out of our frame of reference, they can help us see what's possible. I call this being stuck in our mud. Sticky, thick, up to your knees mud that is your life when you're operating in self-protective patterns, fear, and overwhelm. It's where we tend to land when our ego spends too much time in the driver's seat of our life. Our growth is learning to zoom out on our own life while surrounding ourselves with a community that can support us when we can't see the mud we're in or a way through.

As I reflected on being love, joy, strength, light, and grace, I wondered how God saw me. Remember, I had been functioning with the belief that I somehow landed outside the cover of His grace. I started to ask this question—"Lord, help me see me the way You do." This question was THE question for me in this season. And He showed me. He spoke through my army. His army. I continually asked the question, and He continually reminded me. When a challenge showed up, I would ask, and He would answer. When fear showed up, I would ask, and He would answer. When imposter syndrome or not-enoughness showed up, I would ask, and He would answer. Do you know why? Because when we ask, He shows up. And when we are receptive and open, we can receive a response. "Keep on asking, and you will receive what you ask for. Keep on seeking, and you will find. Keep on knocking, and the door will be opened to you"

(Matthew 7:7). Notice how active this is? Keep on, keep on, keep on. Continually ask. Continually seek. Continually knock. He shows up for us, but we must be active participants. We must also be seeking and listening, and staying in receiving mode.

Until this point, where I started to actively work at being receptive and allowing Him to change the way I think, He couldn't get through all the noise I was creating in my life, through the chaos and the busyness and the proving. He couldn't get through my roadblocks because I wouldn't let Him. I was so committed to my not-enoughness that He had to let me fall. He had to let me run out of steam so that I would let go of enough of me and my control to make room for Him.

And as I continued to listen, He continued to affirm through the people around me and experiences in my life that He saw me as not only love, joy, strength, light, and grace, but He also saw me as worthy. As powerful. As His daughter. I began to see myself as chosen. Full of stillness AND fire. A fierceness. A wholeness. And an innate enoughness.

For the first time, I began to believe that it was ok to like myself. Maybe it was even ok to love myself. And that was a big deal because when you don't love yourself, you don't take good care of yourself, it's hard to live the life you're on this earth for from that place. Not to mention that it's hard to let people love you if you don't believe you're worthy of love. I get it. That was me. No boundaries and burnt out. Not living a life of fulfillment. Maybe this lands for you. Maybe you've bought the story that you're not supposed to like yourself or love yourself, that somehow it equates to being selfish or self-centered. But God loves you, and He wants you to love His people, including yourself.

CHAPTER EIGHT

WHOSE STORY ARE YOU LIVING?

PART ONE: SHOULDS AND NOT GOALS

"I was in a box with expectations and obligations that someone else built and I bought."

To step into who God says you are, you will have to step out of who other people say you should be. And to step into what He calls you to be and do, you have to step out of other peoples' stories for what your life is supposed to look like. That can be challenging when you've built parts of your life, or your entire life, around what you thought you were supposed to do, instead of building it around what God tells you to do. I built my whole life that way, around supposed to's and should's.

When I finished high school (though we could trace this back further) and I was trying to decide what to do with my life, I made a decision based on what I thought would be perceived as successful, a pre-existing standard, a standard that I moved right into. I was success-chasing. I was gauging my worth, decisions, choices, and the things I moved towards by other people's expectations, or at least what I perceived those expectations to be. I picked my university program because there was an interior design minor. I thought interior designers were looked-up to. They were interesting. It was something that would be viewed as special. It was aspirational. When I look back on my efforts to prove that I'm enough and on my career and burnout, here's what's clear—I wasn't living my own story. I was in a box with expectations and obligations that someone else built and I bought. When we buy someone else's "box," we pay for it. There is a cost.

As it turned out, I didn't become an interior designer (hello not-enoughness!), but I did end up building a real estate business that functioned entirely around showing up for people at the expense of myself (hint: that's a cost) because that's what was on my checklist for enoughness, and that's what I thought success looked like. I chose not to take care of myself because I was so focused on making everybody else happy. I was over-committed to making my family happy, making my husband happy, making my extended family happy, making my friends happy, and making every client happy. I had completely drained myself from giving so much of my power away to other people's expectations that outside affirmation had become the source of my value. I built no boundaries. I didn't even know what a boundary was. I had low confidence, and when confidence did show up, it was for short spurts followed by a deep dive into self-judgment. I felt like a complete and total imposter in my business. I had so deeply bought into everyone else's shoulds for me and so thoroughly attached my identity to executing those shoulds that I lost myself in the process. How's that for the cost of buying someone else's box?

Right through to the age of 35, I was busy. My calendar was always full. My to-do lists were always unfinished and growing. I was constantly comparing and checking—am I enough yet? I was looking at who society said I needed to be, who I thought my in-laws wanted me to be, what kind of wife I thought my husband wanted me to be, what I thought my peers wanted me to be... and assigning all of that to ME. Carrying it all, thinking I could make people happy. As if I had that kind of power.

But when I hit my wall, when the burnout was too great, and when the cost got too high, I re-evaluated. As ego-boosting as it was to win awards and have people ask how I was accomplishing all I was accomplishing, I knew that I didn't want what I had. To be clear, I wanted my family and my marriage, but not in the capacity that I was showing up for them. But I didn't want the chaos, and I didn't want the business, even though it was "successful." Don't skip over that. I built "success," and I didn't want it.

As my shift into understanding who I am started, I slowly opened up to a deeper relationship with God. I'd always known He was there, but it was more of an "I'll call you if I need something" relationship rather than a daily connection and dependency. I told Him that I couldn't hold it together anymore. I couldn't figure it out on my own. I felt broken. I opened a bit of space for Him, and He filled in that space. But the space was still pretty small. I'm what you might call a recovering micromanager. I wanted to control everything. I held it all tightly. I worried about what could go wrong. While I had opened up a little space for Him, the rest was filled with control, worry, scarcity, and fear.

I was making really good money, but I didn't feel grateful. I was liked, but I didn't like myself. I even fit in at this point for what felt like the first time, but it wasn't filling me up. It wasn't true belonging. I had checked off a lot of tick-boxes on those checklists that came with the story I bought into, enough that people saw me as successful. And that was what I wanted. Right? What I'd been building for ten years in business. It was what I'd been building toward over a lifetime of trying to fit in and be perceived as enough.

There were parts of the business that I did enjoy, people I appreciated, opportunities that I was blessed with, and ways that I curated the business to be more in line with who I was created to be, and yet... Here I was, having reached the point of what I thought I wanted and now knowing that it wasn't actually what I wanted. It was just what I was supposed to want. Looking at life as a bigger picture, I realized that it wasn't sustainable even though I had moments, blips, or flashes of fulfillment, and I didn't want unsustainable. This period of my life built me, and I'm grateful for how the Lord used it, but I didn't want this big picture, and I knew it wasn't all He had for me. Which meant that "What am I supposed to want?" came up against "What is it that I do want?" and "What is it that He wants for me and from me?"

This meant I had to ask the questions. "What do I want for my life, and where is God leading me?" When I first asked that question, all I had was confusion. It's easier to talk about what you don't want when you're feeling stuck, so I went to that space as a default. I didn't want to be tied to my phone. I didn't want to be in reaction mode all the time. I didn't want to feel anxious. I didn't want the financial ups and downs. I didn't want to feel like there was something else for me. And I really didn't want to know that I was doing nothing about it.

These are called Not Goals, a concept I learned from Andy Stanley in a sermon called "Winning." He explains them this way:

> "A Not Goal is... I'm not going to be like him. I'm not going to be like her. I'm not going to be like my dad. I'm not going to be like my mom. I'm not going to parent like they parented me... You're going to set Not Goals and Not Goals are not enough because Not Goals are not wins. And you will be inclined... to blame and compare yourself through life especially when you begin to feel like... in any arena of life you're not winning, you'll blame and you'll compare, and the problem may be [that] you never decided what a win was to begin with." [14]

A Not Goal is the opposite of a goal, and it's representative of what we don't want. If we don't define what we do want, we will default to putting our focus on what we don't want, or in Andy's terms, we won't focus on something that feels like winning but will instead be caught up in blame and comparison.

One of my other favorite ways to look at this is "Where focus goes, energy flows," this is classic Tony Robbins. His view is this:

> *"Energy flows where attention goes. To get what you really want in life, you need a clear goal that has purpose and meaning behind it. Once this is in place, you can focus your energy on the goal and become obsessive about it. When you learn how to focus your energy, amazing things happen. You get insights that weren't available to you before. You run into people who seem magically put in your path to help you. You overhear conversations or stumble upon resources that further your plan. That's the secret of how energy flows where attention goes...What happens when you're always picking out flaws or paying attention to the negative aspects of life? [You're] committing to staying in a dark headspace, [and] it means you will get more negativity because it's what you're concentrating on." [15]*

To bring it together, whatever we focus our attention on tells our subconscious mind to look for more of that thing. It's as if we create more of it, and essentially, we do. We give so much energy and focus to what we don't want that we filter out other data and opportunities outside of that focus. It's like putting on horse blinders. We see what we are looking for. There is a reason that God tells us to "Fix your thoughts on what is true, and honorable, and right, and pure, and lovely, and admirable. Think about things that are excellent and worthy of praise" (Philippians 4:8). If we aren't looking for the good things, we will miss them even if they are right in front of our faces. We can miss Him even if He is right in front of our faces.

Horse blinders are great if you're focused on the right things. The key is to focus on what we do want and what He tells us to focus on so we can look for that data and those opportunities. Then we can start to create a different outcome. What I actually wanted was to be present with my kids and to be able to sit on the floor with them and be playful. I wanted to know that what I was doing with my life mattered. I wanted more freedom. More God connection. More joy in my marriage. To be able to breathe.

To figure out what you want and create space for God to lead, you need to first step out of all the shoulds. Because it's clouding you. Filtering your life through the lens of what everyone else wants will never give you what you want. It will never fill you up. So what is it that you do want?

PART TWO: SUCCESS BY OTHER PEOPLES' STANDARDS

*"If you didn't build it, and God didn't
confirm it, it's not yours."*

Asking what we want is a starting point. Then we have to redefine and begin to own what comes from asking the question. And let me tell you, figuring out what I wanted was the easy part. Detaching from the identity of "I'm Juli, and I'm an amazing Realtor with a half-million-dollar company" was a big deal for me. All that proving had provided me with steady hits of affirmation, and affirmation happens to be my love language. And, because I bought into other peoples' shoulds and society's shoulds, I was living someone else's story. I put myself into boxes that were never meant for me. God didn't call me to real estate. He allowed it. He allowed me to go on my detour, and then He built me on ramps back to His calling for my life.

I had to redefine what success was to get clear on my purpose. My real estate success was success by other people's standards. It was success according to society's standards. It was success according to the world's standards. If it had been my standard of success in the first place, I probably would have been happier. Look, it doesn't matter if you're a stay-at-home mom, work in a corporate job, or a car mechanic. Wherever you show up in life, there is a standard (or something you perceive to be a standard) of what success looks like. But if you didn't build it, and God didn't confirm it, it's not yours. It's time for a new standard.

Also, success is not work-specific, role-specific, or assignment-specific. Success needs to be defined in the context of your entire life. Your calling is holistic. How you show up in one place is how you show up in every place. You are one person interacting in multiple environments, and there isn't a different essential you for each space. You are you everywhere. And that's both exciting and scary because whatever is impacting one area of your life impacts them all.

Aiming for success is good. Setting and achieving goals is good. God made us to work. He purposed us for it. Before the fall in the Garden of Eden, Adam and Eve worked. Proverbs 6:9-11 (TPT) talks about this. "So wake up, sleepyhead. How long will you lie there? When will you wake up and get out of bed? If you keep nodding off and thinking, "I'll do it later," or say to yourself, "I'll just sit back awhile and take it easy," just watch how the future unfolds! By making excuses, you'll learn what it means to go without. Poverty will pounce on you like a bandit and move in as your roommate for life."

So work is good, but when we aim for someone else's version of success, we are headed away from God's version of success that He created for us. And often, someone else's version of success doesn't consider our whole life, skills, talents, gifts, or calling.

When you lean into other peoples' shoulds, you drift away from yourself. You give those shoulds your power because you are actively giving more value to outside perceptions of you rather than giving it to your integrity with yourself. Being out of integrity with yourself gets in the way of your calling. MISALIGNMENT GETS IN THE WAY OF YOUR CALLING. It creates confusion. And the enemy loves confusion. The unseen forces that we battle don't want you to live your purpose. Remember that. But you were not put here to live in someone else's box of expectations and shoulds. You were put here to be bold and courageous, live His purpose for your life, build His kingdom, and be love.

CHAPTER NINE

WAKING UP

PART ONE: THE PURPOSE-LIFE CRISIS

"The purpose-life crisis is defined by a pervasive sense of "what I have in my life right now is not enough."

If we don't take time to redefine success and we continue to live someone else's story, we will inevitably end up here—the purpose-life crisis. We're talking about this before we work on clarity of your purpose because you need to understand what's at stake and what being in a purpose-life crisis means.

When I hit my wall and decided something had to change, when I realized that I didn't want what I had created, the key underlying theme was that I wanted to live fulfilled. I wanted to be excited about my life. I had a deep desire to do something that mattered. To make a massive impact. To create lasting and sustainable change. To live in a world with more compassion, kindness, love, empathy, and justice. I wanted to save the whole world – that may be a stretch, but I knew I had people to serve. And I also knew that I wasn't doing it.

To the outside world, I'm sure some people would have argued with me. I'd built an entire company culture around giving back and being generous. I had created my success with these questions in mind, at least subconsciously: How do I look successful to my peers? And how do I look successful and not too egotistical to my friends and church family? Also, if I'm being transparent, how can I make sure God continues to give me this financial abundance and be deserving of the life I have? While it looked good, I still wasn't connected enough with what He was calling me to do. I wasn't connected enough to build a life that was fulfilling and aligned with who He created me to be.

I was in the middle of what I call the *purpose-life* crisis, which is defined by a sense of "what I have in my life right now is not enough." I see it in people with success who aren't fulfilled. People with what they were "supposed to have" but don't want it. People who want to know they are doing something that matters, but deep inside know they're living small and that there is an elusive something else out of their reach.

In essence, that's the mid-life crisis, right? But it's not reserved for the ages of 35 to 55. This is not about how old you are. It's about God calling you up and allowing you to reach the point where you'll truly turn to Him and say, "Ok, it's your turn. I'm ready to live your story for me."

So much guilt shows up in this space. We are told that we should always be grateful. We should always be joy-filled. We should always be courageous and bold. But we aren't always grateful, are we? I sure wasn't. And it's challenging to be joy-filled when you know, at some level, you are operating in opposition to your Father. Cue guilt. I can't believe that I'm here. Cue shame. What's wrong with me?

But that guilt and shame keep us spiraling. This is where the "I am's" come into play. Where you say, "Hold up, self. I am love, joy, strength, light, and grace. I am His. Let's step out of the guilt and the shame and do something to shift this. Let's walk our way back to ourselves and to Him, one step at a time." That's the first step out of the purpose-life crisis.

To build some momentum out of the purpose-life crisis, you need context on two concepts that underpin its existence: The Comparison Trap and the Capability Gap.

PART TWO: THE COMPARISON TRAP

"There is no room for us when we live in comparison, and we don't leave much space for God either."

One of the common manifestations of not-enoughness is comparison. As someone who has lived trying to measure up to other peoples' expectations and to fit in, I've struggled with comparison for nearly my entire life. Not only is comparison the thief of joy, but it also is the thief of compassion.

Claiming our enoughness and reclaiming our too-muchness, requires us to get curious about where we are leaning into comparison and to redefine who we tell ourselves we are supposed to be. If you make a list, you might be surprised by what shows up. I know I was. Here's a list of who I have caught myself comparing to:

- Other people in my field.
- Other people outside my field.
- Women who are prettier than me.
- Women who are taller than me.
- Women who are smaller than me.
- My husband.
- Better Christians.
- Better helpers.
- Imaginary people.
- Ideals of people.
- Instagram perfect people.
- People with bigger followings.
- People who fill events faster.

- People who fill courses faster.
- People with happier children.
- People with bigger houses.
- People with bigger wallets.
- People with smaller wallets.
- People who are better activists than me.
- People who are more resilient than me.

And...

- Who I tell myself I'm supposed to be...

This last one is the key. Because comparison isn't actually about other people, it's about who you tell yourself you are supposed to be. The rest of that list only plays a role if we let it. It only has power if we give it. Ultimately, it's about the expectations and standards we hold ourselves to. And when we get curious about what and who we are comparing to, it further reinforces that we are so often living into someone else's story, someone else's definition of success. Not to mention that our comparisons and the standards we are adopting for ourselves often contradict each other.

Here's an example, people with bigger wallets and people with smaller wallets. There is no winning here. I'd look at friends who were happy with their smaller homes and content in their day-to-day, who had fewer material possessions, and wondered if I deserved what I had. Was I stewarding my resources well? Was I living a life God would be proud of? Maybe I'd be happier and more content with less. And then I'd get to work and see luxury cars in the parking lot or walk into expensive houses and wonder who I had to be to have a kitchen like that, a view like that, or a lifestyle like that. Both situations completely contradicted each other. They were both robbing me of contentment because I was robbing myself of contentment. I had adopted opposing standards and believed that I needed to be both humble and modest to be a good Christian and, at the same time, that I needed to be financially successful and rich to live a life that others would look at as good enough. Where in that was what I wanted? Where in that was what I was called to? Nowhere.

There is no room for us when we live in comparison, and we don't leave much space for God either. It's like saying, "Hey Jesus, I'm going to go give all my attention and energy to fighting with myself and holding myself to impossible and opposing standards, so I'll check in later when I'm failing, and if you could somehow fill in the gaps so that this struggle will make me happy in the end, that would be great."

That is not how it works. We must return to what He wants for us, which is good and perfect. Given that we are created in His image, do you not think that what makes Him happy will also make you happy? Do you not think that what makes Him satisfied will also satisfy you? When Jesus talked to the woman at the well, He told her, "Those who drink the water I give will never be thirsty again" (John 4:14). It wasn't that she needed to continue to search for worldly things to satisfy her needs and desires. All she had to do was step into surrender and receive. Jesus had prefaced this with, "If you only knew the gift God has for you and who you are speaking to, you would ask Me and I would give you living water" (John 4:10).

If you only knew the gift God has for you. Never thirsting. That's what's available for you and for me. We just have to choose to be available to receive it. That's leaving the purpose-life crisis behind. That's what stepping out of comparison looks like. That's what stepping out of living other people's stories looks like. That's what stepping outside of other people's definition of success looks like. It's allowing Him to fulfill you. In other words, to fill you up. It's allowing Him to fire you up about life and to give you freedom from comparison.

PART THREE: THE CAPABILITY GAP

"There is a higher-level part of us than the ego that reminds us that we are here to create an impact that only we can."

When we let go of comparison, we can focus on our own journey and our own path. We can focus on becoming who we were put here to be. And then, we can start to close the gap that underpins the purpose-life crisis. The gap that drives the inner knowing that the person that you're capable of being is not reflected in your day-to-day reality.

I call this the capability gap, the space between where you are and what you know you're capable of. There's a tension here because you know that you're capable of something beyond what you're producing right now, beyond what you're living right now, beyond your way of being right now. But you're still here. There is something God has put on your heart and is pulling you toward and calling you to. He has created a path for you, for this moment in time, and because you're reading this book, my guess is you're out of alignment with it.

Every single one of us has a calling. Every single one of us is here on purpose, with purpose, and for purpose. And there is a higher-level part of us than the ego that reminds us that we are here to create an impact that only we can. That voice tells you that the world needs you and that God, your Father and your Creator, has a plan for your life. This inner higher part of us opposes the ego. This inner higher part of us is God in us. It's Holy Spirit territory.

Understand that you have two options when it comes to the capability gap. You can choose the growth journey, step through fear and say no to overwhelm (aka go to battle with your ego), or you can stay the same.

When you stay the same, your ego remains in control. You will continue to experience this internal dissonance and tension because you're out of alignment with yourself. More importantly, you are out of alignment with God. You're fighting your intuition instead of fighting your ego. And that in and of itself causes us to be exhausted and overwhelms us.

Not to mention that staying the same is choosing to say no to God and His plan for you. It's choosing to prove to yourself that you're unworthy, choosing to operate in fear, and choosing not-enoughness.

But you have NOT been given a "spirit of fear and timidity" (2 Timothy 1:7)! You have been given a spirit "of power, love, and self-control" (2 Timothy 1:7, ESV). The fear is not yours. Our birthright as Jesus followers is to let go of the fear and own the power that is ours. You are more powerful than you know. You are more called than you know. Stop claiming the fear and hanging on to it as if it's a part of you.

Let's have a real talk moment here. As I've become clearer on who He says I am and who He calls me to be, my ego fed me this story. "What if you're not as called and as powerful as you think you are? What if people look at you and see a fraud? You need to know more, do more, and be more before you even think about owning these dreams in your head. Stages? Singing? A book? That's practically putting proof out in the world of your not-enoughness." And you know what, that story in a previous season of my life would have worked.

But I know who He says I am. I know He says that I am love, joy, strength, light, and grace. I know that my Father says I am His powerful daughter. I know that He has specifically told me to go speak and teach and sing and write and preach. I know that He has been building me for something I do not yet see. And I know that He has given me a spirit, not of fear and timidity, but of power, love, and self-control. Which meant I had to detach from the old, untrue story and figure out what was actually up.

My ego had distorted reality through the lens of not-enoughness, but as I stepped back into my enoughness being settled, I realized that my question was this—"What if I am as called and as powerful as He says I am?" Ouch. That meant I had to show up in alignment and integrity with someone who is called and with someone who is powerful. That was the scary part, and for my ego, it was an entirely new way of being. There was no certainty of what that would look like. There was no definitiveness about the path from my perspective. There was no control because this path required me to surrender it. Of course, my ego would fight this.

And yet, Romans 8:28 says that "We know," catch that, WE KNOW, "that God causes EVERYTHING to work together for the good of those who love [Him] and are called according to His purpose for them." Stepping into my calling and stepping onto my path comes with a guarantee. That my God, my Father, my Comforter, my Provider, and my Healer will cause everything to work together for MY good. And not only that but according to His purpose for me.

Do you know what that means? All your shortcomings, detours, failures, and times that you look back on and feel shame means He can (and does) use ALL of them to work together for your good when you love Him and step into the purpose He has for you. That's what Him building a path and making it straight looks like. And then, He shows us the steps through the capability gap. His word is a lamp to our feet and a light to our path (Psalm 119:105, NIV), so not only is He creating a path for you, not only is He making it straight, but He is installing streetlights to keep you clear and moving forward. He is determining your steps (Proverbs 16:9).

This used to make me uncomfortable. I want to determine my own steps, thank you very much. But do you know what happens when I do that? I jump onto my own bumpy path. It's not about robbing us of our free will. It's about guiding us to a fulfilling, freedom-filled, and passion-filled life. A life that is fired-up, fulfilled, and free.

CHAPTER TEN

LIVING YOUR PURPOSE

PART ONE: WHY AM I HERE?

"Your purpose is for you, but it's not about you."

So why are you here? I grew up believing that this was the question no one seemed to be able to answer, at least from a societal perspective. In my experience, that's total and complete nonsense. You're here on purpose, with purpose, and for a purpose. God put you on this earth at this time intentionally. And now that you have a sense of your essence combined with an understanding of what your ego has been up to, you can step toward clarity on your "why."

At the beginning of my growth journey (when I really got intentional about it), "I discovered the audiobook of Simon Sinek's Start With Why. This was in my first period of really questioning whether I would stay in real estate. It was a "salesy" and transactional industry. I attempted to follow other real estate agents' maps to build my business, but none of them fit. I was running up against conflict with who I was and what I valued, even though I didn't have a conscious understanding of that yet. I must have read and listened to that book cover-to-cover three times back-to-back. It was my first introduction to the idea that I could build my life, my company, my client journey, and essentially every box in my life in a way that worked for me. Maybe, just maybe, I could define success in one area by myself.

Initially, I missed the point, though. I looked at my life and saw these themes of belonging and protection that consistently underpinned what I valued, how I operated, and what and who I was drawn to. But I narrowed my personal why to "helping people." That is more of a coping mechanism for me than a why statement. Over time, though, things became clearer by leveraging Simon's framework of contribution leading to impact [16] and then tweaking it and revising it. As I became clear on who I was and could use that as a filter, I could see how my identity flowed into my calling.

Hang with me there for a minute. Your identity exists above the boxes, representing the essence of who you are. We've covered that. The same goes for your purpose. Your purpose and your calling are not titles. It's not coach, nurse, mom, grandpa, husband, executive, or volunteer. Those are assignments—boxes along the ground. Your purpose exists above that too.

I looked at being love, joy, strength, light, and grace and started to ask God the question, "What do you want me to do? How does being these things at my core mean that I get to show up in my life? Where does that mean you're leading?"

Here's where I landed: I'm on this earth to empower others to find their fire, trust themselves, and live their purpose so that they can live their most fulfilling and impact-creating lives as their whole and authentic selves. That means a lot to me, but it may not mean much to you. And that's ok because purpose statements aren't marketing statements. They're for you. They remind you what the path forward looks like. A purpose statement is a tool in the toolkit that will help pull you through the hard days. Through the moments when your inner critic is just too loud. Through the interactions with others when you feel completely judged. Through the attacks, the criticism, the confusion, and all those moments when you want to give up. Your purpose reminds you of God's call on your life. Your purpose is a source of clarity and courage.

Clarity on your purpose will come through your essence, your identity. And it will be influenced by everything God has been using to build you and threads that show up through your life. Belonging and protection are threads that have shown up throughout mine. Finding my fire, which is my expression for reclaiming too much, standing in my power, and boldly and courageously letting God flow through me, has been a thread through my journey. Learning to trust myself, and ultimately the Holy Spirit in me, has been a consistent struggle and story in my journey. Living my purpose, and learning to identify it and move toward it, is something that I can see in play as far back as I can remember. And ultimately, what I wanted was fulfillment, to do something that matters, and to be loved and accepted as my whole self, which is where the last bit of my purpose statement comes in. My journey with this has prepared me to walk others through their journey. It was God building me and getting me ready to serve.

Hear me on this. Your purpose is not about you. It's for you, but it's not about you. It's for you because it brings fulfillment. It's for you because it gives you clarity. But it's about something bigger. It's about moving forward as God's kingdom. It's about being love to our neighbors. It's about a bigger work that He is doing through us collectively. It's not about you.

PART TWO: DEFINING YOUR PURPOSE

"When you understand your purpose and that you exist for something bigger than you, freedom arrives."

I bet you're curious by now and wondering what your purpose is. Maybe you're pulling together themes. That's good because this is where we hit pause and deep dive into getting clarity on what you're here for. So grab your pen and paper because it's time to explore.

First, remind yourself who you are. Because within your identity lies the parameters of purpose. It always ties together. You may also want to look at words you highlighted in the "I am" exercise that didn't make it through to your shortlist, as there is often guidance here.

Second, we are going to look at six areas. Take your time to brainstorm through these and write down whatever comes to mind.

1. WHAT HAS BEEN AMAZING IN LIFE?
- What fires you up and gets you excited?
- What are you passionate about?
- When have you been the most fulfilled or happy?
- In hindsight, when have you felt the most aligned with your "I am" statements?

2. WHAT DRIVES YOU NUTS?
- What makes you angry?
- What frustrates you?
- What triggers you?
- When do you feel the most protective or driven to create change?

3. WHERE ARE YOUR THEMES?
- Look back at your most potent memories and experiences. Are there themes that you see consistently showing up?
- What are the consistent threads (challenges, wins) in your life story?

4. WHAT IS THE CONTRIBUTION YOU CAN MAKE?
- What are your gifts?
- What are you skilled at?
- What are you a natural at?
- What are you passionate about?
- What are the things that people say you are great at?
- How do people feel around you?

5. WHAT IS THE TRANSFORMATION YOU CAN CREATE?
- What change could exist in the world if you make the kind of contribution you've listed in Question 4?
- What is possible?
- What could happen?

6. WHAT IS THE IMPACT OF THAT TRANSFORMATION?
- What could change for the people or causes you serve if they see the transformation from Question 5?
- What is possible?
- What could happen?

From there, we get to start narrowing down and pulling key themes together. Here's the basic framework:

I [contribute my talents and skills and passions] to [create transformation in people/causes/environments] so that [there is a particular impact of the transformation].

To use my purpose statement as an example:

I'm on this earth to empower others to find their fire, trust themselves, and live their purpose so that they can live their most fulfilling and impact-creating lives as their whole and authentic selves.

The contribution is empowerment. The transformation is finding their fire, trusting themselves, and living their purpose. The impact is living their most fulfilling and impact-creating lives as their whole and authentic selves.

A purpose statement often evolves, and it demands returning to, praying over, and being flexible with. This example took reviewing a handful of times before it felt right. Before it landed. And it will likely be tweaked and adjusted over time. The essence of it, though, is there, and like "I am's," this becomes an anchor. It becomes something that you can return to daily and build a practice around that helps bring you out of ego territory. It's a tool that will help you step through your fear. Because when you understand your purpose, you can focus on the people and causes you are called to impact.

When you understand your purpose and that you exist for something bigger than you, freedom arrives. Because if it's not about you, you have nothing to prove. You don't own your purpose. God does. You're not the one proving anything. God is. And He CAN. Your calling and purpose are not being about you mean that all your fear, confusion, and resistance become irrelevant. That's all you stuff, ego stuff. Do you still experience it? Of course, you do. But it's not about your ego. It's not about your fear. It's not about your scarcity mindset. And when you start to see all of that, success starts to look different. You have a new measuring stick, and it's wrapped up with a bow to understand your purpose.

Repeat after me, "I am God-sent and God-purposed, and I have nothing to prove."

He is sending you, which means He's got you covered. Ephesians 2:10 (NIV) says, "We are God's handiwork, created in Christ Jesus to do good works, which God has prepared in advance for us to do." If He has prepared this path for you and this purpose for you, and if He makes you worthy, then doesn't it follow that He built you for this? Of course, it does! And let's be clear, whether you feel ready or not is irrelevant. Do people like what you're doing? Not your business. Do you feel like you're enough? Also, irrelevant. God is freeing us of our commitment to fear and proving, and He's asking, "Do you trust me yet?"

PART THREE: THE SECOND LENS

*"Because I now understood what I was measuring against
(my essence), it meant that I needed to get my everyday
life into alignment with what I was being called to."*

The "I am's" lens of who you are is your first to look through and evaluate life by. Calling and purpose, that's the second lens. From there, you start to see what is aligned for you. What fits and what doesn't in the context of where you give your time and energy? Which of the boxes stay within this context? Which ones don't? What gets added? How much time and energy, or in other words, how much of the essence of you goes to each box that is still in your lineup on the ground?

I realized, looking through my lenses, that real estate was not the most aligned space for me to show up in. Was I really helping people find their fire and trust themselves? Was I helping them live their purpose by helping them buy and sell homes? That was a huge NOPE.

Because I now understood what I was measuring against (my essence), it meant that I needed to get my everyday life into alignment with what I was being called to. I was on a bypass route to my own path, and it was time to get back to the one He made for me.

Let's be real, though—FEAR showed up. Fear because I had a lifestyle I didn't want to let go of. Fear because I had so intensely wrapped my identity up in being a successful real estate agent. I had a family to support, bills to pay, and I didn't want to disappoint anyone.

I fought hard to maintain my status quo. My ego fought hard to keep me overwhelmed. I didn't feel qualified, and I didn't feel ready.

Something unexpected pulled me through it. And I bet it's not what or who you expect. It was you. Yes, you reading these words. In realizing that my calling wasn't about me and my old measuring stick, I also realized it was about you and your transformation. It was about taking the love, courage, peace, joy, and compassion that God, my Father, had given me and giving it to you. It was about the transformation that existed for you. He had a plan to work through my life, and I wasn't going to get in the way of what He wanted to do and still wants to do in and through your life.

I'm not going to pretend it was easy. It wasn't. It was challenging because I had well-ingrained habits of proving my enoughness, and I had to let them go. I had to redefine myself. But He kept asking me, "Do you trust me yet?" And He kept telling me, "Go."

CHAPTER ELEVEN

GET ON YOUR PATH

PART ONE: MAKING YOUR PATH STRAIGHT

"We often carry so much of ourselves into the journey that we take unnecessary detours."

Throughout the bible, there are references to the path we are called to, to God making straight your path. Even to Him creating multiple paths. Your purpose will help you narrow your focus and get in tune with what He is leading you toward. But we often carry so much of ourselves into the journey that we take unnecessary detours.

When I first connected with the idea of being a coach, I thought to myself that I could do that and real estate. I had this desire to change the real estate industry, to make it more relationship-focused, and I latched onto what seemed to be the obvious solution. More accurately, the safe solution. "I can be a real estate coach!" I can just see God shaking His head and pulling out a facepalm, but He humored me. I needed the small transitional step to test out a new space. To let go of some of my identity attachment to "real estate agent." To make sure it was safe. This felt like a major transition to me. I started dreaming about what coaching agents would look like, structuring packages, building out marketing campaigns, and shifting my networking focuses. I landed three big speaking opportunities right away, and generally, opportunity seemed to be all around. A few months later, I launched my first program. It was a six-month coaching group for real estate agents to help them build businesses that served them instead of having businesses that ran them. I had high hopes. Twelve people were going to rush in and sign up. It would be a big success and a full group. Well, that didn't pan out. It was crickets for weeks.

I was crushed. "What is going on, Lord?" What had gone on was that He gave me some direction, and I said, "Ok, I got this. I'll call ya!" And off I went to build my thing. My idea of success. My copy of how I saw others reaching success. I didn't really ask Him. I felt defeated, but He allowed my defeat so that He could call me back to Him. So we could co-create, and I could see that what He had was better.

I kept at it and eventually signed four people. Less than I had hoped, but it turned out to be a beautiful number for me to work through my own becoming process as a coach and a mentor.

A few months later, I ran another launch for entrepreneurs. I thought I'd cracked the code, and it would be a slam dunk. Again crickets. "Ok, Lord, what the actual #*$%?" I leaned into Him a little more this time and said, "Maybe you just don't want me to do this. So tell me what you want me to do. I'm done pushing my agenda." I shut down the marketing, turned off the webpage, and then the surprise came. Within a week, enough people had reached out saying they wanted to sign up that I ran a seven-person program, more "successful" than my first program, with less push and hustle. I thought, "Ok, Lord, you're telling me something. Trust you more, and don't try so hard." Over the summer, I ran the program, and my client list continued to grow. He was providing. He was building it with me. And he was doing something interesting through it. He instilled in me that my focus and passion were identity and purpose work; it wasn't about real estate. It wasn't about entrepreneurs. It was about people understanding who they are and what they're here for.

He told me what the straight path looked like that He was building for me. And He was telling me to leave real estate behind.

He said jump. Did I listen? Nope. Instead, I leaned on the advice of people in my life, saying I would make more, and it would be easier if I launched one more round of real estate programs and then slowly transitioned into a more identity-focused space. It was one last detour into the world's way of doing things, and I took it. I put my faith in people. I had clarity on my purpose, but I didn't quite trust Him yet. I wasn't ready for that faith leap.

PART TWO: HOLD YOUR NOSE AND JUMP

*"He was putting me back on the path because it was time,
and there was more on the line than my comfort."*

Not only was He giving me direction on what the straight path was for my coaching business, but in that same season, He was telling me to leave real estate entirely. Let me tell you, my ego didn't like that very much. All the voices in my mind came in and said, "Who do you think you are?" "What makes you qualified to do something else?" I heard an old coach in my head when I would say to her, "I couldn't do what you do," respond with, "yeah, maybe not." I had so thoroughly tied my value to being a successful entrepreneur, a successful real estate agent, and a successful member of my industry that the concept of walking away to do something else was nearly paralyzing, except I was in a purpose-life crisis, and I had learned enough about myself to know that I couldn't continue hiding in real estate. I knew it wasn't my purpose. And I knew I couldn't keep doing things that were status quo.

I had to start untangling all of that. God told me what the next step was, but I was scared. I told Him, "I can't make the same money." I thought that maybe I needed to hit some financial targets first. Or maybe I needed to find someone to sell the business to. Maybe I needed to just give it some more time. Maybe it would just kind of happen. Maybe this... maybe that... maybe, maybe, maybe. I'm an expert story-maker. My favorite story was this one: "What if people think I'm crazy?" My business was bringing in $500,000 a year, and God asked me to leave it behind. Truthfully, it wasn't even that I was concerned that other people would think I was crazy so much as I thought I was crazy. I worried about how to transition in a way that felt safe and how to do it in a way that wouldn't put too much pressure on my husband or would potentially threaten my marriage. How could I make this massive life transition while still completely and entirely controlling every move and not trusting God's plan? I was battling wits with the Creator of the universe. Whatever story you could come up with was rolling around in my head. But He kept at it. "Do you trust me yet? Go now. Just jump."

I've learned that God doesn't usually ask me to transition over time slowly. He says, "GO NOW!" And I argue. And He says, "GO NOW!" And I argue some more. And then He shows me who's boss. The houses I thought I needed to sell first, He put up roadblocks. The business I thought I needed to sell, He blocked that too. It was as if He was telling me, "It's go-time, and you can move, or I will move you." While a part of me still struggles to believe that I'm chosen and that people are assigned to my voice, I know that He was done waiting for me to feel ready, and we were moving forward whether I liked it or not. He was putting me back on the path because it was time, and there was more on the line than my comfort. It was like He was yelling at me, "Over here! This way! I've got you! Trust me!"

I called my partner and asked what it would take to have her take over the business, and I walked away. I quit real estate. I disbanded the team. I sold off what assets we had. I shut down my ten-year business. And do you know how I felt? Not how you might expect. Here's what I expected – FEAR. And resistance. And hesitance. And anxiety. But what I actually experienced was relief. I was peace-filled, hope-filled, and so incredibly relieved. This is what is available to you when you get on His path. Relief. Peace. Joy.

My real estate business was keeping me distracted. It was keeping me from fully stepping into my calling. And the cost of staying there, as made clear by my purpose, was you, the people who were ready for my help, my skills, and my support in their journey so they could create more impact in their lives and the lives of the people around them. There's a ripple effect to everything we do, and it goes beyond anything we'll ever see. There are impacts from someone being open to change and being open to a new self-awareness that flows out beyond anything we'll ever hear about or see. But the impact exists. And God knows.

Walking away from my business was a massive up-level. Instead of playing small, instead of dimming my light, instead of trying to make everyone comfortable around me, I focused on God tapping me on the shoulder, saying, "Go."

Getting on His path was transitional. I had to navigate some bumps in getting there because I was moving from my path to His. From a bumpier path that ran alongside the one He had intended for me to His smoother and straighter path with streetlights installed. So many of those bumps were caused by me trying to hold onto parts of my old identity. Some of them were there because God still had work to do on my trusting Him. He had to let me take a few more hits and show up for me through it before I'd fully get on His path. God doesn't do things to hurt us. That's not His character. He does, however, allow us to experience the consequences of our actions. That's a good parent.

For example, instead of focusing on the identity and purpose work, I launched the one last round of real estate programs I told you about earlier in this chapter. I enrolled twelve clients between two programs – what I'd discovered to be my perfect group size. It was a success. It looked like the advice I had received from others was good advice. The detour was looking good from my perspective. There was a problem though – what I was doing didn't authentically reflect me anymore. And that ended up impacting my ability to hold clients. Not a single client had left a program early up to that point. But this time, things started to shift a little as a few people dropped out. It was an ego hit every time—the cost of my detour. I started asking, "Am I not good enough? Am I not worthy? I left my business Lord; what else do you want?" I felt so entitled to a smooth ride because I felt like I'd sacrificed so much, but I still wasn't listening.

It was still early in the Covid-19 pandemic, and I hadn't taken a break to this point. I hadn't slowed down my schedule; I hadn't taken weeks at home realigning to my values. So many people around me had talked about the beauty in the rest and reset, but I had taken all my energy when real estate got quiet in lockdowns and funneled it directly into my fledgling coaching business. I got sick, and things finally stopped. Jesus stepped in and took me out of my doing. It was the first time I slowed down in years. And in the slow down, in the anxiety of not being physically able to do things, He was there. He was so present. So tangibly and emotionally supportive. And He reminded me of who I was and where to focus. He said, "Step into me. Love your precious children. Love my precious children. You are not fragile. You will not break." I saw that even in my taking control from Him over how I was building my business, He was working and putting pieces in place. I realized that the longer I tried to make all these plans and control outcomes, the bumpier it would be. That's the deal. It's not about your plan. Your plan will not go the way you want it to. Frankly, if you listen, it will be better than you could ever come up with on your own or do your way. And it will be bumpier than you want it to be if you don't listen.

Interestingly, when I got sick and God was reinforcing that it was time to step away from the specific focus on real estate to pursue this identity and purpose focus, my team had been working on a summit and a podcast launch. The Becoming Ourselves Podcast and The Becoming Ourselves Conference. Neither of them had anything to do with business, entrepreneurship, or real estate. They were passion projects, and they were both purely focused on identity. They were focused on becoming our authentic selves and, in a way, coming back to God. The podcast had been a clear call from Him. He inspired the conference. And as I looked at these opportunities while trying to come to terms with the tension of what I was now seeing as misalignment with my groups that were focused on real estate, I realized that these two projects were actually a pure representation of my calling. That I'd made this big "hold my nose and jump" transition out of my own real estate business, but it was only the first jump. God had been curating a parallel path off to the side of the one I was on, and He was waiting for me to catch up. My next jump was to step out of real estate on all levels and step into the space He had been building me for.

Fear showed up again. Fear of being judged. Fear of not being able to make money. But I knew this time that I needed to get on His path and off of mine. Getting onto it meant I would have to deal with some fallout. It was a business pivot. It would take me back toward start-up because I would have to shift how I marketed, attracted, and served clients. But I made a choice. I would trust Him this time. Really trust Him as much as I could. It had been a year since the launch of my business and only a couple of months from the end of my old business, and it was time to fully step into the work He had for me.

We don't always realize this about "hold-your nose and jump" moments. There isn't ever just one. It's layers and levels as we go through our journeys. As we grow and as we get deeper and deeper levels of clarity, there is always another jump. And when we don't jump the first time, He builds another on-ramp to our path. He keeps calling. You haven't missed out. It's not too late for you. Our God is abundant, and there is something that He has for you. That is not a permission slip to wait because the work He has for you was purposed for YOU. And trust me, the waiting gets bumpy.

Isaiah 43:19 says, "For I am about to do something new. See, I have already begun. Do you not see it? I will make a pathway through the wilderness. I will create rivers in the dry wasteland." There may be a dry wasteland to your eyes, but He is working even when we can't see it. And He is making it work together in a way that is better than what you can imagine. It's better than what you know to hope for. Stay there for a moment and breathe it in. Part of you knows that's true.

I remember first hearing this quote from Jeff Foxworthy and it resonating deeply in my soul. "You haven't lived until you've had a few hold-your-nose-and-jump moments." [17] It turns out, he's right. It's never just one.

CHAPTER TWELVE

THE REAL WORK

PART ONE: THE GROWTH CYCLE

"Being able to borrow other people's faith in me when I lose mine and having others speak over me has given me the permission and the freedom to explore new territory."

Let's recap. We've tackled enoughness, too-muchness, the ego battle, the who are you questions, whose story you're living, and why you're on this earth. Take a deep breath because this is where the real work begins. We've been creating a new awareness and building a new set of lenses to look at life through. And awareness is great. New lenses provide the opportunity to show up differently. Which means it's time to do just that. It's time to do something with the awareness, the clarity, and the lenses. It's time for growth and integration. So what does that process look like.?

Well, your path may be straight, but growth is bumpy. Why? EGO! (Surprise!) This is where your intentions are great, but you're likely to regularly get in your own way. That's because you're stepping out of your comfort zone, where your ego wants you to remain all the time. Instead of staying comfortable, you're choosing and moving into growth. Your ego would call that change, and remember, your ego doesn't want change because change isn't "safe."

Think of your growth journey like the front end of a bell curve. There is this flat area at the beginning, and then you climb, gently at first and then more steeply. The flat part is rest and integration. Often people want to wrap that space up with the label of plateau, a place where it feels like you're doing nothing or that you're not moving forward. But in reality, this is where we take whatever lessons we've learned and who we have become in our last phases of growth and make them a sustained part of ourselves.

I like to think of this plateau of rest and integration as the space where our ego can let go of its death-grip on who we used to be (that version of us that it fought so hard to maintain) and reattach itself to the new version of us. It's as if our ego says, "Oh, ok. I have enough proof in this new space that we'll be ok. I have enough proof that we are safe and secure here and can get our needs met here so I can get on board with this new version of us."

Integration is a space where we solidify our identity foundation. Where we can rest in the knowledge of who God says we are, be still, and wait for His next direction to move. It's a space where we can breathe and get ready for the next phase of our growth journey, the next climb up the curve. It's where we reinforce our foundation and grow roots that will support our next transformation. It's also a space that has some level of comfort inherent in it, and that's necessary. It's tough to rest from a place of discomfort. It's even more difficult to get your ego on board from a place of discomfort.

What happens if you don't integrate the new parts of yourself, sit with the lessons, and create habits around your new way of being? What happens if you try to skip over giving your ego the space to attach to your new way of thinking and your transformation? Well, you'll try to climb the growth curve, but you'll skid back down like a child trying to climb a tree that doesn't have branches. And your ego will perceive failure. It will grab hold of that and say, "See! I told you it's not safe! I told you that you'd fail. Just stay here. It's good enough."

By contrast, when we build a solid foundation, we have something to build on as we climb that next growth curve and step more fully into who God calls us to be. This integration and rest phase is just as vital as the growth climb. Personal and spiritual growth works in a pattern: we climb, and then we integrate, and then we climb, and then we integrate. We must be intentional about each season of our journey, intentionally connected, intentionally surrendered, intentionally curious, and intentionally listening.

When you enter the growth phase, moving up on the bell curve, you're entering into a place of challenge, a season of stretching your edges. This is where I've found my ego to be the most active. This movement through the capability gap is uncomfortable because our ego is again fighting to maintain its existing frame of reference. Remember, it thinks a bear might jump out from behind a minivan. So it is going to do its ego thing and throw overwhelm and inner critic judgment at you. If you're on God's path, you're also fighting the enemy who doesn't want God's purpose for your life to be fulfilled. The growth phase is where you become even more dangerous to the enemy.

This growth phase requires you to operate from a place of continual choosing. You get to choose how you're going to show up and who you're going to be day-by-day, hour-by-hour, and moment-by-moment. Jesus talked about continual choosing when He said, "If any of you wants to be my follower, you must give up your own way, take up your cross daily, and follow me" (Luke 9:23). Daily! As in over and over. And Paul references that, "Our spirits are being renewed every day" (2 Corinthians 4:16). Our crosses may look like burdens, yet we can be comforted in knowing that our Father God renews our spirits daily. Continually. He's not asking you to walk this journey or choose to keep growing and stretching and becoming a more powerful and authentic version of you alone. He's not asking you to become more like Him alone.

Look, our Lord Jesus knows that we will falter. He knows we have tough days. He knows we will come up against resistance. So He's been clear in this daily piece. Staying in alignment with Him intentionally, giving Him our time daily, and being consistent over time is how we step through a growth curve. It's by continually choosing to look through the lenses of who He says we are, what He has called us to, and then asking how that requires us to show up. Asking and then doing, executing on it. It's also massively important to surround ourselves with the right people, build support tools, and put ourselves in spaces that both call us up and remind us who we are when we forget.

In this season of being called to be bolder about my faith, I've been intentional about surrounding myself with people who already do that, who are an example to me. This is crucial because it gives me some form of proof that I'll be ok on the other side of this growth curve—you're welcome, ego—and it keeps me out of a space where I think I know it all or I've done enough growing. Being able to borrow other people's faith in me when I lose mine and having others speak over me has given me the permission and the freedom to explore new territory. It helps me catch my own patterns when I start to get in my own way (and faster than I used to) because those self-protective patterns are so default that sometimes I don't see them. But the people around me often can because they aren't in the proverbial mud with me. They aren't in my stories or my experience. They aren't looking through my lens, which means they can maintain what we call observer status.

PART TWO: OBSERVER STATUS

"The Enemy uses everything from imposter syndrome and overwhelm, to trauma, to our desire for an easy fix to pull us off our path and get in the way of establishing the Kingdom of God on the earth."

We've spent so much time talking about our ego so that you can start to recognize when yours is showing up and throwing a fit or trying to drive. And when you recognize it, you can zoom out and detach yourself from it. This is taking on observer status. It's like big, grown-up you watching little, four-year-old you throwing a tantrum and saying, "That's interesting. I wonder why they're doing that?" Cue the ego battle hugs.

When I was still in real estate, and before I got any of this clarity about who I was or what I was here for, I had a nightmare client. Let's call her Dina. Dina and I got along great at first. We shared interests and would have the most interesting conversations when we looked at properties. It appeared as if she was an ideal client for me. Partway through the process, though, it was as if a switch flipped, and she went from ideal to full-on harassment, shaming, and generally blowing exceptionally minor challenges into world-ending explosions. She was someone that I had gone above and beyond for. Someone I cared about. Someone that I was committed to working through a major life transition with. I received five-page-long emails that attacked my character and my competence. My career was threatened. And I was eight months pregnant. The situation was bad, the timing was bad, and everything about it shook me to my core.

Looking back, I can stand in complete integrity and know that these attacks were unfounded and completely inappropriate. However, at that moment, my pattern was to believe whatever people said about me, to spiral into shame. I still believed I was unworthy of belonging and protection. All my old emotions from being bullied as a teenager came up in my face. Bertha was yelling. I was living in fear and anxiety. I was completely consumed by this confirmation of my not-enoughness. I was angry, but I questioned what could be true about what she was saying about me. I was incapable of stepping out of the emotion and being logical about the situation. My ego had me in its grips, and there was no way out. I lacked the ability to step out of the chaos and observe it. Eventually, the situation was resolved, but it left trauma in its wake.

Fast forward two years, I'd reached a point of clarity about who and whose I am and an understanding of how my ego functions. I was having a conversation with a woman who was mutual friends with someone who had stopped responding to my messages. I'd checked in to see if this friend was ok and asked this mutual friend to say hi and that I hoped all was well. This woman accused me of not showing up for this friend and went on a tirade about what she perceived as a failure on my part. It felt a lot like Dina all over again. My ego wanted to default to my old patterns and see this through my not-enough lens. But this time, I could see what was happening. While my ego desire was to fix it, make everyone happy, people-please my way through, allow myself to be thrown under the bus, and believe what was being spoken about me, grown-up me wasn't having it.

I believe in self-responsibility, but self-responsibility does not mean owning other people's stories. It does mean looking at your role in a situation and evaluating if there is something that integrity requires you to do. It is, however, never your responsibility to own someone else's trauma or victim space. Their reactions are not your responsibility.

To the best of my knowledge, I had shown up as love and maintained healthy boundaries with my friend but was still thrown under a bus. That's not to say that my defaults and her defaults or that our brokenness as humans didn't lead to some kind of hurt. I recognize that is entirely possible. She has a different lens, background, and life experience than me, so it's not mine to determine whether she was hurt. What was mine was to step back into who He says I am and get curious. "Ok, Ego. What's up? What's true? Let's zoom out and look at the facts. Let's look at the realities of the situation. Let's ask God how He wants us to handle this. And then let's do what he says."

I recognized that this was not between me and this acquaintance I shared with my friend. It was between me and my friend. That initial conversation was over—no more middlemen. I reached out and offered to talk to my friend and hear her side, to hold space and understand where she was coming from, and understand what her experience and expectations were. It was never responded to. That was fine because I knew I'd done what I needed to do. I'd extended my hand. I'd shown up in integrity, and that's what was mine to own.

Because I had zoomed out, prayed, and looked at this objectively, I also knew I had a boundary to set, and I had to get clear on what was going to keep me on my path. Where was God leading me next, and what did that require? He very clearly directed me to cut off communication and all relationships that linked me to these people. Whether He asks me to maintain that permanently is not up to me. It's up to Him. But at this point in my journey, it was toxic for me to be carrying these relationships and the tension that existed in them. This is important – it wasn't that the people were toxic. It wasn't about them at all. It was about where God had me. It was about my current level of ability to manage my patterns in this relational tension. It was about the impact of the calling on my life of staying connected. This time, I could see what was happening and what was triggering me from an observer space. I could talk to my ego, work through the stories, and stand confidently in my power and enoughness. That was a major win, as much as the loss of connection hurt.

Someone reading this needs to hear this—you may not always be right, but you are not, by default, wrong. You are not, by default, less than everyone around you. You are not required to adopt their perspective. And you are not required to hold space for people that are being sent to take you out of your power. This is where we get into Ephesians 6:10-12: "Be strong in the Lord and in His mighty power. Put on all of God's armor so that you will be able to stand firm against the strategies of the devil. For we are not fighting against flesh and blood enemies, but against evil rulers and authorities of the unseen world, against mighty powers in this dark world, and against evil spirits in the heavenly places."

First off, we have nothing to fear. "If our God is for us, who can ever be against us" (Romans 8:31)? Second, guess what one of the primary strategies the Enemy uses is? Ego. The Enemy uses everything from imposter syndrome and overwhelm, to trauma, to our desire for an easy fix to pull us off our path and get in the way of establishing the Kingdom of God on the earth. Even these women that I had to cut ties and create boundaries with were used by the enemy against me to keep me from stepping forward. Again, it wasn't about them. It's not that they were under some demonic hold. It was about how the enemy knew I'd spiraled before into the stories of not-enoughness that have kept me small. It was insidious and subtle. The enemy was weaponizing my ego because he knew what to use against me. And he knows what to use against you.

If we try to do life in our own power, he will get under our skin. But if you're operating in God's power, this is what happens next. We can get to a point of watching for and seeing this all in action. And then we can put our armor on, laugh, and say, "Get out, Satan. I know whose I am and what I'm called to. You have no authority here. You have no power here." Then we step confidently forward on our path. Proverbs 10:22 (TPT) says, "The one who walks in integrity will experience a fearless confidence in life." That's the target. Fearless confidence. Not our trauma driving. Not ego winning the battle. Not the enemy weaponizing our ego and our self-protective patterns. Instead, fearless confidence, laughing without fear of the future (Proverbs 31:25). That's our birthright.

CHAPTER THIRTEEN

HOLDING THE LINE

PART ONE: I'M NOT THERE YET

"The real work is showing up daily, reminding ourselves who we are and whose we are, and choosing to be available to let Him work."

Western culture tells us that we need a quick fix and a fast solution. That life can be one and done. But as far as the growth journey goes, this is the furthest thing from the truth. You're becoming yourself, and that is an ongoing journey. There is no proverbial there to get to. You will always have a next growth phase. You will always have another layer of ego stories or self-protective patterns to work through.

This part has always been a challenge for me. I'm what I call a warp-speed eight human. I can be impulsive. I move quickly. I have been known to struggle to slow down, rest, or be still. I've so often looked for that quick fix. The boyfriend that will make me whole. The outfit that will help me fit in. The product that will organize my business for me. The book that will help my toddler develop easy bedtime sleep habits. The retreat that will once-and-for-all fix my not-enoughness problems. The coach that will fix my money issues.

There are two problems with this. One is that I'm putting my faith in the wrong place. I heard Andy Stanley preach on this many years ago, and he's written about it in his book Irresistible. He reminds us that if we put our faith in a person, a product, the church, and even the bible, it will all fail us. But Jesus, He won't fail. He is the only one and the only thing we can put our faith in that will never fail. [18]

Coming from a place of putting my faith in a lot of other places, I couldn't agree more. I've experienced church hurt and trauma. I've misinterpreted the bible and seen it weaponized. I've watched as self-described Christians completely miss the point of what Jesus came to teach and show us about love and justice. I've put my faith in coaches, speakers, teachers, books, programs, prophets, and products... and ultimately, they all fail because they are all representative of humanity, which means they are imperfect and flawed.

And that's the key piece, isn't it? Because we are flawed, we won't just "get it right." We have to work at getting it right, and we have to be clear on what getting it right means. All of that is a process. As I write this book, I'm not at some proverbial place of there or done, where I have everything worked out and figured out. I still struggle with my humanity daily. But I am committed to the process of letting God transform the way I think, letting Him work in me and through me.

We spend our entire lives attaching to our patterns and self-protective mechanisms. We view the world through them. As powerful as God is, He is also a co-creator with us. And the fact that He's given us free will demands that we are active participants in His process and choose the process. But because we are flawed, we need to continually return to the process. This is continual choosing work—minute-by-minute, hour-by-hour, day-by-day. Our acts of obedience require active obedience. And this is why clarity on who we are and our purpose becomes so fundamental and foundational. It's a leverage point with ourselves that we can use to create an opening for Him to work through.

The real work is showing up daily, reminding ourselves who we are and whose we are, and choosing to be available to let Him work. He keeps telling me, "Just show up and let me do the work." We think that to be worthy or enough, we need to be done. We need to be there. But there is no there. And where we are right now is where He can use us. God isn't asking us to live for tomorrow, or next year, or decades from now. He's saying, "Be here with Me now. Let Me love you now. Let Me guide you now. Let Me take care of tomorrow and next year and thirty years from now. I know what that will look like. And if you stay on the path, if you can be still and be present, I will do greater things through you than you can plan for yourself. I will guide you through the storms. I will fill you up when you need filling. I will light a fire in you. I will give you the peace and the joy that I've been over here holding out to you and waiting for you to receive. Just let go. Let go of the pressure. Let go of the push. Let go of the hustle. Let go of the fear and the worry and the strain. Let Me love you and let that flow through you to the people in your life."

As a recovering micromanager and worrier, I'm not going to pretend that this is or has been easy. Frankly, it's been a battle. This is why we talk about ego battles first before we get here. I've had to contend with mine daily. I will continue to contend with mine daily. And I don't do it alone. I show up, and I let Him work. That's the choosing. I still ask – "Help me see me the way you do, Lord. Help me let go of my control. Help me learn to rest in you. Guide me back to where you are. Surround me with your army. Teach me to trust you."

In his letter to the Philippians, Paul speaks about living in responsive obedience. "When I was living among you, you lived in responsive obedience. Now that I'm separated from you, keep it up. Better yet, redouble your efforts. Be energetic in your life of salvation, reverent, and sensitive before God. That energy is God's energy, an energy deep within you, God Himself willing and working at what will give Him the most pleasure..." (Philippians 2:12-13, MSG). This has been so powerful in the most recent phase of this journey. I'm really leaning into the concept that my growth, becoming myself, and journey through fear to freedom is a co-creation that requires me to listen, receive, and then act on what He tells me. That's why this book exists. That's why I jumped careers. And He has fueled me with the energy to act.

PART TWO: THE IMPOSTER INVITATION

"Instead of building barricades between ourselves and our callings, we can take a sledgehammer to imposter syndrome and step over the rubble."

When we step into this work, one of the most common struggles with our ego is imposter syndrome. A feeling that we are not enough for, equipped for, worthy of, or capable of what we are stepping into. What if people knew? Imposter syndrome is a soulmate to comparison, Bertha is its voice, and the enemy leverages it to keep you out of responsive obedience. We typically think of imposter syndrome as a negative, and if we let the ego drive, it can be. But as believers and as Jesus followers, it's actually a permission slip. It's something that the enemy tries to weaponize, and do you know what that means? You're on the right track.

When God gave me the call to jump out of my real estate business, I was convinced that people would think I was crazy. I was worried about finances. I walked around assigning the stories in my mind to everyone around me: my husband, my staff, my friends, my colleagues, my family... Who was going to be disappointed? Who had told me I couldn't? Who had an attachment to my current level of success? It was imposter syndrome and fear central.

But Imposter syndrome shows up in every single up-level. Every time I've tried something new. Every time I've been on the ledge of a personal growth breakthrough. Every time I say yes to His next call. Every. Single. Time. As I started to see the pattern, this occurred to me—the discomfort exists because I'm on the right track. That's just my ego freaking out because I'm changing again, I'm reaching a new level, and I'm stepping through my capability gap.

This is key. First, we must know who we are and what we are called to be. We must be clear on who is leading because imposter syndrome combined with God's leading defines the invitation to keep going. Imposter syndrome can show up when we are putting up roadblocks and staying on our own path too. That's not a permission slip to stay out of alignment. But when we are allowing God to lead, imposter syndrome showing up is a win. That's a celebration moment. It's a confirmation that the enemy tries to use as a deterrent.

Instead of building barricades between ourselves and our callings, we can take a sledgehammer to imposter syndrome and step over the rubble. Suck it, enemy. You have no power here. Sometimes stepping past imposter syndrome is easy. Sometimes it is a continual choosing. Ultimately, it's about trusting that our Good Father has us in His hands, trusting Him and His path, surrendering to the journey, and not looking at what other people's journeys look like along the way because they aren't yours. It is about what you make the journey mean about you. What story do you assign it? Does failure leave room for the enemy to sneak in and take you out? Or do you allow yourself to say, "Ok, Lord, what do I need to take from this and learn? What are you asking of me next?"

Imposter syndrome + God's leading = winning at life.

PART THREE: LEVEL UP YOUR PEOPLE

"This growth journey will, without fail, require you to level up your people and shift the dynamics of your existing relationships."

Some people in our lives will adapt and be generally supportive of our shifts toward living the life we are called to and built for. The reality, though, is that not everyone will. I won't sugar-coat it. That part is hard and makes it really tempting to step off the path when conflict arises.

While boldly living your purpose in the power of who God created you to be can function as a permission slip for others to live their most powerful and authentic lives, our lives can also function as a mirror that reflects the shortcomings of others. And sometimes, there isn't a willingness to adapt or meet us where we are. Sometimes we have to let people go that are no longer in alignment with us as we move in the direction we are called to. That isn't necessarily a them-thing or an us-thing, but purely a we-aren't-on-the-same-page-enough-for-me-to-be-supported-by-maintaining-this-relationship thing.

I was asked in an interview about how my friendships have changed through my journey over the last few years. How many of them still were intact? My answer was not many. I'll caveat and say, with all the moves and changes, combined with my self-protection patterns about potential rejection, I've never been one to have long-term friendships. As I look back, though, and witness the journeys of the people I serve, some people will not honor our new boundaries. Some people's values function fundamentally in opposition to ours. Sometimes we grow to love ourselves and start to recognize toxic relationships in our lives. Regardless, this growth journey will, without fail, require you to level up your people and shift the dynamics of your existing relationships.

When I hit the last burnout of my real estate career and discovered who I was, the community of women I was surrounded with changed, and new people came into play who were also committed to their own growth. There was a resonance in that space where we all pulled each other forward. We believed in each other and the potential that existed for our lives and businesses. I saw collaboration over competition, which I thought was a fairy-tale concept until then. They saw me, and I saw them. And I thought I had found a sisterhood that would last a lifetime.

And then that container, in its formal capacity, ended. Most of the women from that space and I drifted apart with only social media to keep us connected. As I write this, I have one close friend from that group of twelve humans that has remained a consistent part of my life. I say this to highlight that the Lord will send you people on your journey. However, His intention may not be for them to stay long. And that's ok. That's healthy. People-pleasing or trying to hold yourself in a space that creates tension or roadblocks between you and who He is calling you to be isn't an option anymore.

And frankly, some relationships demand more of a fight than others. My marriage was my most important fight. In all the turbulence of my shifting, combined with a global pandemic, we had to continually come back to each other. By contrast, relationships with real estate colleagues with whom I had no forced connection dropped off rapidly. When we visited our parents, figuring out how to be my authentic self was worth giving energy to and building boundaries around. People that I was only friends with because I was carrying the relationship, not so much. In none of these circumstances was this an "I'm better than this relationship" energy, but instead one of "does this serve the direction I'm going?" And, "Is this healthy?" We can let go of people and still love them. We can drift or actively cut ties from a place of love.

We need to take a minute and ask this because from a perspective of maintaining compassion and cutting it out with the story-making our egos love so much, you need to understand it. Why the turbulence? It's because we all function according to "social contracts." And as we change, we break those contracts. Let's use my example of going to the crazy "woo woo" retreat. When I got home, I felt like a new person. I was excited. I was joyful. It was a completely different energy. I expected everyone around me to be as excited and revived as I was. But the reality was that my husband, who had taken care of our littles for five days and was tired, didn't have the same experience as me. Duh Juli. I felt deflated and frustrated. He felt like I was over the top (that's my perception anyway). It was tension.

Here's what I didn't understand. We had a pre-existing social contract. My ego was used to how my husband showed up, behaved, thought, spoke, worked, etc. I had a current frame of reference for what to expect of him. My ego was latched onto that (it likes safe and the same, remember). My husband's ego also had an attachment to how I showed up, behaved, thought, spoke, worked... you get the idea. So when I came home "different," I pulled the consistency and predictability rug out from under his feet.

I had a choice – I could be upset with him because I was convinced that he could be more supportive. Or I could choose to take a step back and remind myself that this tension was my fault. I'd triggered it because I was intentionally changing how I showed up. Instead of being frustrated, I could be compassionate and give him a chance to adjust. I could check in and see what he needed. In reality, he was 100% willing to support my growth – something I'm beyond grateful for –

but he needed a minute to catch up with me and let his ego recognize that the new "social contract" we'd have was good and safe too.

Take a look at your life. Who have you been frustrated with when you've been the one that changed? Where is there room for more compassion? And when has someone else's change triggered you? We inevitably end up on both sides of this relational tension that comes with change.

Sometimes we will work through the tension and redefine the contracts. Sometimes people will change and grow with you. Sometimes they won't. Remember this – God has built us for community. In owning our power, battling our egos, and staying on the path, He does not intend for us to be alone. He intends for us to be called up and supported. Prayed for and reminded who we are when we forget. He wants us to be in a healthy, wise community with shared values. That's a fundamental space for you to grow in. He built us to grow together. Those desires that He has for us will sometimes require that this community change.

Allow Him to tell you where to let go and where to hold on. To guide where you need to build boundaries both with yourself and others. To lead you into what to say yes to and when to say no.

Allow Him to send you your army for your journey. That may be a church community. That may be a therapist or a coach. That may be a new friendship or a mentor. Be available and ask Him for clarity.

Allow Him to use you as part of someone else's army, to be a supportive friend, a forgiving spouse, or a praying neighbor. To volunteer or build a business or ministry that lifts the people He loves.

Be intentional about where you spend your time and energy and who you give it to. Spend time in prayer. Test out journaling and meditation if you don't already use them as tools. Get into nature and listen for Him. Listen to the kinds of podcasts and read the type of books that bring you closer to your Heavenly Father.

Seek out the kinds of people who will call you up in this next season, who will inspire you, who can mentor you and guide you, and who can support and empower you to live fired-up, fulfilled, and free.

CHAPTER FOURTEEN

FAITH OVER FEAR

PART ONE: TAPS ON THE BACK

"God loves you with a never-stopping, never giving up no matter where you go or what you do kind of love."

Our faith is our lifeline as we do the real work. Through all the bumps on the growth journey that come, through the ongoing ego battle, and against all forces of the enemy, God stands with us. And He always has.

When I was about seven, I had my first faith crisis. We'd gone on a family vacation to the East Coast, where my dad's family is from, and we went on a ferry to Grand Manan Island. I don't remember a lot about the trip, but when we returned home, I started having nightmares. Dreams that my brothers were falling off the boat into the ocean, and I had to save them. Sometimes I did. Sometimes I didn't. I also started having dreams about battles between light and dark. I can't remember the exact details of them, but I remember being so afraid. It continued for months.

I'd been raised in the church, and I'd spoken aloud that I believed in God by the time I was three. And I continued to in case I hadn't done it right. But at seven years old, dealing with all these dreams that I didn't know what to make of and that were so incessant, I hit a breaking point. "God, you've gotta fix this." I was questioning whether or not He was real. I wasn't sure what I believed. And one night, I'd had enough.

As I lay in my white wooden bed that my dad had built in my rainbow-wallpapered room, I gave God an ultimatum. "If you're real, tap me on the back." This wasn't an I'm being funny, and I want attention moment. This was an I am dead serious, and this will determine the course of my faith permanently kind of moment. I turned over and buried my head in my pillow, not sure what to expect. And I felt a firm tap tap tap. I flipped over, and no one was there. My parents weren't hiding on the floor. My brothers were asleep. And I knew. He's real.

This moment has brought me back so many times when I felt like an outcast as a child and believed that I was owed better by God. When I was bullied for two years by my former best friends, and no one seemed to be able to make it stop. When I was dumped by a boyfriend whom I thought I was going to marry. When I was a 20-year-old stepmom contending with how my life would never look like the nuclear family that society promised and expected. When I lacked community. When I was miserable in my job. When my business was failing. When my church was failing. When I was failing. In all those circumstances when faith seemed so hard, I'd ask myself, "Do I really believe this? Really?" there was this little moment, this seed, and this remembering that He tapped me on the back.

As I thought about this experience and writing this book, something occurred to me. He had this planned the whole time. He'd chosen me so early. And you need to know that too. You're chosen. Whether you had a tap-on-the-back moment or not, He chose you. Before you were even born, He chose you. He continues to choose you. He loves you with a never-stopping, never giving up no matter where you go or what you do kind of love. I say this to my kids all the time, "No matter where you go or what you do, I will love you, and you will be mine." That's how He loves. And He always has.

He knew I'd fight Him. He knew I'd say no to some of His calls. He knew I'd struggle. And He knew exactly what would build me, my faith, and my character to a point where He could use me to reach you.

God tells me to be filled with fire, be a voice for Him, and speak for Him. He tells me that He doesn't need it to be all polished and perfect but that He will speak, and those who speak His language will hear. He tells me to rest in His hope. He wants that for you too. He's asking you to trust Him.

PART TWO: OPEN HEART, OPEN ARMS, OPEN HANDS

"Get in position."

Moving forward on His path for you means you need to adopt the right posture. This word used to confuse me. What do you mean posture? I stand up straight. But that was missing the point.

Posture is defined as both a noun and a verb. As a noun, it reflects the way you carry your body, and the way you carry your body is a reflection of your mindset and your heart space. Are you confident or egotistical? Are you empowered or victimized? Are you controlling or in surrender? As a verb, posture reflects how you take action on that mindset and heart space. It reflects your perspective, your way of thinking, and your frame of reference.

Stepping through fear and into freedom has brought me into a particular posture more than once. Physically embodying this posture, just like with pattern interrupts, sends a signal to your subconscious and helps remind you of who you are.

I call this the power posture. Open heart, open arms, open hands. So what does that look like?

Open Heart:

An open heart requires vulnerability and trust. It requires us to choose to be transparent, to be in surrender. Because what's the opposite? A closed heart. A heart with walls. The opposite of an open heart is self-protection – blocking love from coming in. A heart with walls blocks compassion from ourselves, God, and others. Having an open heart as a posture allows our Lord to work in us. It allows Him to break down our walls to grow us and expand us. Vulnerability means that things may hurt along the way, but that's also required. We cannot experience love without the risk of rejection or loss. We cannot build walls to protect ourselves and, at the same time, be in a space of receiving.

The reason we start with the heart in this posture is that it's where love lives. And it's where I feel God the most strongly. Our heart posture impacts and flows through to every other space. An open heart requires trust, and our posture is an act of obedience. An open heart also allows us to be in flow and alignment with God as He has given us love not only for us but also so that we can be love to others.

The bible refers to the heart continually. That "He searches our hearts" (Romans 8:27, NIV). "We know how dearly God loves us because He has given us the Holy Spirit to fill our hearts with His love" (Romans 5:5). That we are to "Guard [our hearts] above all else, for it determines the course of [our lives]" (Proverbs 4:23). And "Christ may make His home in your hearts as you trust in Him" (Ephesians 3:17). The heart is the gateway. If the gateway is open, He can work in and through us. And He wants to. He's faithful like that.

How faithful? It's right here–"For the mountains may move, and the hills disappear, but even then my faithful love for you will remain. My covenant of blessing will never be broken, says the Lord who has mercy on you" (Isaiah 54:10).

Let's drill down. The mountains that have stood for thousands of years may move. The hills that have outlived generations may disappear. But that is all irrelevant because he says, "MY FAITHFUL LOVE for you will remain regardless of what unlikely things may happen." We must allow His love in. We must allow Him to do the work in us and break down our walls so that we can receive it. So that we can rest in it. So that we can depend on it and allow in the grace and the peace and the contentment that also comes to be abundant in us. When we wait for the answers to our prayers, when we wait for His promises, when we wait for challenges to pass, we can do it in His arms, surrounded by love. And then we can open our arms to the people around us and the people He sends us.

Open Arms:

Open arms are a symbol of both power and grace. The story of the prodigal son is perfect here because as he returned home from wandering off his path, his father was there to welcome him back home with open arms. The father had every right to shun the son who had demanded so much and not listened to his father's wisdom. But despite all the son's shortcomings, his father welcomed him back with a never-failing, no matter where you go or what you do, I will love you and you will be mine kind of love. He had the power to do otherwise, but He chose not to use it. He chose grace. Powerful grace.

This open arms posture reminds us of the grace that our Lord Jesus has for us and how we are called to be like Him. It's also a posture that reminds me of what Jesus did for us on the cross. Stretched out and yet, still powerful. Still grace-filled. On this journey, we will come up against challenges and enter into moments when we need to be powerful. To set boundaries, speak against what is wrong, and challenge people we encounter. Standing in powerful grace will be a requirement of walking out your calling. It's a way to reflect our loving Father, who has grace for us, who is with and in us, and who is the source of our power.

We fight that, don't we? It feels like something we can't handle or manage on our own. And that is exactly the point. He doesn't intend for us to hold it alone. He intends to use us as a conduit. Open arms are a signal—we are choosing yes. We are choosing to be who He says we are. There is nothing to fear. "The Lord is my Light and my salvation—so why should I be afraid" (Psalm 27:1)? Pick a different battle. Stop fighting God and go to battle with your ego. Go to battle with the enemy who weaponizes the ego and has no authority. Take all the courage you need from a God who walks with you.

Open Hands:

Taking courage requires the open hands part of this posture. Open hands are symbolic of surrendering. And the surrendering leaves you in a position to receive what He has for you. It's choosing to be available. It is also reflective of letting go. Letting go of the need to control all things. Letting go of making plans and over-attachment to who the world says you are. Letting go of guilt, of shame, of your commitment to being a victim, of your not-enoughness, of your stories, of your should's, and your comparison. Let go and give it to God. Make room to receive His gifts and His direction. Say, "It's all yours anyway, so you hold it."

Open hands mean we hold outcomes and plans loosely. We pivot easily. We aren't holding on so tightly to things that we can't move when we are told to move. We are free to be and do what is next on the path. We are also free to grab hold of the opportunities God sends to us.

Being Rooted:

The last piece in this posture that God has revealed to me is all about rooting into Him. Stand while you practice this. Feel the ground under your feet. Colossians 2:6-7 says, "And now, just as you accepted Christ Jesus as your Lord, you must continue to follow him. Let your roots grow down into Him, and let your lives be built on Him. Then your faith will grow strong in the truth you were taught, and you will overflow with thankfulness." That's a pretty awesome promise. Follow, root, build your foundation on Him. Then you'll have an abundance of thankfulness. Here's how thankfulness is defined – "the feeling of being happy or grateful because of something." [19] Being rooted is what keeps us "strong and immovable" (1 Corinthians 15:58). It helps us stand firm in our faith journey and be courageous and strong (1 Corinthians 16:13).

Open heart, open arms, and open hands is a posture where God can flow through you. You can't be angry or weak in this posture. Go ahead and try. You can't be selfish in this posture. You can't build roadblocks and walls from a place of open heart, open arms, and open hands. The path ahead of you is clear. There may be attacks from the side, but we are held and guided, protected and strengthened, supported and loved when we walk behind the Lord, surrounded by His army, in a posture representative of His power and His grace and His love. And that means we are in a position to do what He calls us to next. Get into position. It's time.

CHAPTER FIFTEEN

LIVING FIRED-UP, FULFILLED, AND FREE

PART ONE: POWERFULLY AND AUTHENTICALLY YOU

"On the other side of your becoming is a life that is fired up, fulfilled, and free."

As we get to the last phase of this journey, I'm thinking about what's on the other side for you. What's the point of this ego battle and reclaiming your enoughness? What's the outcome when you understand who you are and what you're here for? What exists when you show up and do the work to get on and stay on the path?

If you could see me smiling at you right now...

Look, I've seen so many people struggle with purpose and with feeling like their life is mediocre, that this can't be it. I've talked to so many people who don't love their lives. People that feel stuck. People that are losing the battle to overwhelm. I've been that person saying, "Really? What is it all for? Am I not supposed to be happy?" You may be there. You may be wondering if doing the work is worth it. If coming back to yourself and who He says you are is worth it. You might be wondering if you even can—is it in the cards for you?

Understand this. I am not special. I am not unique. I am not outside the bounds of His grace or His plans. And I am on the other side of the bridge that you're staring at, waving you over. Because on the other side is a life that is fired up, fulfilled, and free.

PART TWO: FIRED-UP

"Fired-up is a battle stance, and we're here to fight for what is good and right."

Let's break that down. What does a life that's fired-up mean? Fired-up is power. It's joy. It's clarity on purpose and the impact of your purpose being lived out in the world. It's being excited to wake up in the morning and get to it, whatever your it looks like. It's boldness and courage. Remember Queen Esther? I imagine her saying, "Screw it, I'm gonna go do what I need to do and let God carry me through the consequences." Fired-up is that kind of energy. It's confidence and a reclaiming of our too-muchness. Living fired up means that we embrace the power that exists in our authenticity. It's a place of action. Let's circle back to what Paul said in Philippians 2: 12-14 (MSG) about being "energetic in your life of salvation, reverent and sensitive before God. That energy is God's energy deep within you, God Himself willing and working at what will give Him the most pleasure. Do everything readily and cheerfully, no bickering, no second-guessing allowed." Fired-up is about connecting to that energy and saying, "Ok, Lord, whatcha got for me today?" Because He is working in you, giving you the desire and the power to do what pleases Him. Plus, if we are made in His image, don't you think what pleases Him will also please you? I sure do. I see it regularly on this side of the bridge.

Fired-up is I WILL NOT BE MOVED energy. Paul also told us to "Be strong and immovable. Always work enthusiastically for the Lord, for you know nothing you do for the Lord is ever useless" (1 Corinthians 15:58). In our alignment with our Lord and Father, we can stand firmly in our identity as His daughters and sons. Read that again, because if you're like me, you skim over that stuff. We are daughters and sons of the Creator of the universe. What does that mean about your birthright? He has put us here to powerfully stand as light, as builders of His Kingdom here, as a force for justice, and as living examples of love and compassion. Fired-up is a battle stance, and we're here to fight for what is good and right. Get into position and be on guard. We can stand firm and be courageous. 1 Corinthians 16:13-14 lays this out and adds: "Be strong. And do everything with love."

PART THREE: FULFILLED

"Being fulfilled allows us to show up and be light in the world from a place of overflow."

According to dictionary.com, Fulfilled is defined as a verb. It's an action word. And it refers to carrying out or bringing something to realization, performing a duty, obeying commands, satisfying a requirement or obligation, bringing to an end or completion, and developing the full potential of something. [20] This is interesting because, in conversation, we typically think of fulfillment as the end product, as a state of being or an endpoint.

"When I get here, then I'll be happy." Right? But it takes action to be in that state. And it takes the carrying out of and performance in the context of obeying a command to get there. It takes us moving along the path that our Lord Jesus has assigned us to. It's not a magical "now I'm there" thing. It's a continual action and aligning with Him that brings us into the state of fulfillment, and it's available along the way, not just at a completion point. Not to mention that God's plan for us is bigger than what we see or comprehend, so us determining the trigger point for reaching completion is going to be inaccurate.

Let's break the word down, though. It's full-filled. Full and filled. The definition of full is "containing all that can be held; filled to utmost capacity; complete; abundant." [21] Full is a state of being. Fill is an action. "To make full; to become full" [22]. When we listen and act on what we are called to, we get into alignment with Jesus. And He will fill us with His love, His joy, His peace, His strength, and His courage.

John 15 talks about the metaphor of the vine and the branches. Jesus told his disciples that "as the Father has loved me, so I have loved you. Now remain in my love." Sounds easy enough, right? But there is a how-to that follows. "If you keep my commands you will remain in my love, just as I have kept my Father's commands and remain in His love. I have told you this so that MY JOY may be in you and that your joy may be complete. My command is this: Love each other as I have loved you" (John 15:9-10, NIV, emphasis added). Complete joy! Isn't that what we are after when we think of fulfillment? And love each other. Because your calling, your path, and your purpose is not about you. It's about the people He calls you to love.

Being fulfilled allows us to show up and be light in the world from a place of overflow. It means that He has filled us to capacity and that we have allowed Him to work in and through us. We "do everything in love" (1 Corinthians 16:14, NIV), and since He is love and He is in us, we are letting Him flow through. That capacity also means we aren't draining ourselves to take care of people or be present with them. We give the overflow. We step out of burnout. We step out of overwhelm. We step out of "I can't" and "I don't know." And we step into freedom.

PART FOUR: FREE

"Freedom is surrender without fear."

This is ultimately the point of the journey—living in freedom. This is the other side of the fear-to-freedom journey. Where He asks you, "Do you trust me yet?" and you say, "Yes." Freedom is surrender without fear. Freedom is looking at life and seeing how He has always been present.

When I stepped out of my half-a-million-dollar business, I felt relief. And that was because I knew in every fiber of my being that my Heavenly Father had me. That this was what He called me to. I was stepping onto the path that was assigned to me. And after that relief came challenges. Launches that didn't turn out the way I wanted. Getting sick with Covid shortly after I left the old business. Working through the emotion of holidays that we couldn't spend with family due to the state of the world. The aftermath of a minor concussion for our then six-year-old daughter. Job insecurity for my husband. And financial stress from all of the changes.

In so many ways, I felt like we were in a perfect storm. It felt like chaos was swirling around me, and at times I would get sucked into the swirl. But then I would come back to "I am love, I am joy, I am strength, I am light, and I am grace. I am His. And He has called me to this work. He has assigned me to this path. And He has me." I would imagine myself stepping back into the center of the storm that is life and planting my feet. Saying I will not be moved from this place. No matter what comes, no matter what mountains tremble, no matter what waters rise, I am His, and He has this. And peace would fall. Stillness would come into my soul. I would step back into the power that is my birthright and continue asking, "What's the next step?"

Psalm 46 tells us that God is our refuge. It speaks to how He is with us and that we have nothing to fear. That He is mighty and powerful and that He is a protector. That He seeks justice and that He is always there to help us. I don't know about you, but that is what I need to rest, be calm, let go of the fear, and step into the freedom that He offers me.

Matthew 11:28-30 (NIV) says, "Come to me, all you who are weary, and I will give you rest. Take my yoke upon you and learn from me, for I am gentle and humble in heart, and you will find rest for your souls. For my yoke is easy, and my burden is light." He gives us rest. That means it is available. We don't have to earn rest. We don't have to work for rest. He holds His hands open, freely giving it, arms open to embrace you, and heart open to love you.

Freedom exists through faith. "You, my brothers and sisters, were called to be free" (Galatians 5:13, NIV), and Galatians 5:6 says that faith expresses itself through love. See how this all circles back? We are His. We are set free. Remember? "It is for freedom that Christ has set us free" (Galatians 5:1, NIV). It's what He wants for you. We are called to be love. We have an assigned path to go be love on. We are powerful. We are light and an example to the world. We are chosen, and we are inherently enough. All we need to do is choose. Choose freedom. Choose faith and live our lives in responsive obedience to our Lord Jesus and what He taught. "If you openly declare that Jesus is Lord and believe in your heart that God raised Him from the dead, you will be saved. It is by believing with your heart that you are made right with God and openly declaring your faith that you are saved" (Romans 10: 9-10).

If you're not there yet, consider this an invitation to make that declaration. And if you already have, maybe it's time for a renewed yes. Because that is the source of freedom, anything else will never be complete. And the world is waiting for you to show up on your path, to be love and create impact. To live a fulfilled life. God is knocking—it's time to step through the fear and be your authentic and powerful self.

PART FIVE: BE STILL

"Freedom is surrender without fear."

God gave me this as an anchor in my journey, so as we bring this book to a close, I want to share it with you. I pray it blesses your heart as it has mine.

Be strong and courageous
Do not be afraid or panic because the Lord will go personally ahead of you
Determining your steps
Putting HIS love within you
Working in you
Giving you the desire and the power
to do what pleases Him

Praise Him for His great love
For the wonderful things He has done
Blessing us with stillness
Bringing us safely out of the storm
Calming it to a whisper and stilling the waves
Producing fruit in Him
Providing faithfully a place to land
So let the mountains tremble, and the waters surge, and the fires burn
Let the earthquakes tremble, and the mountains crumble into the sea
For He is our refuge, our strength, and our fortress

Wait patiently, my child
I am working in you in ways you do not yet see
But you will

And they will
I am building you
Helping you be ready to shine for me
To be light in the dark
Giving you power and love and self-discipline
Strength and dignity
Laughter and joy
Wisdom and kindness

Practice
Continually choose me
And you will have peace and be filled with joy

REFERENCES

[1] Henschel, C. (n.d.). The Effects of Parenting Style on the Development of Narcissism. Psykologi & Sakkyndige. Retrieved November 1, 2021, from http://www.sakkyndig.com/psykologi/artvit/henschel2014.pdf

[2] Brown, B. (2015). Daring Greatly: How the Courage to Be Vulnerable Transforms the Way We Live, Love, Parent, and Lead. Avery. P 69

[3] Brown, B. (2015). Daring Greatly: How the Courage to Be Vulnerable Transforms the Way We Live, Love, Parent, and Lead. Avery. P 71

[4] Neff, K. (2011). Self-Compassion. Adfo Books. P.41

[5] Brown, B. (2010). The Gifts of Imperfection: Let Go of Who You Think You're Supposed to Be and Embrace Who You Are (1st ed.). Hazelden Publishing. P.26

[6] Encyclopedia Britannica. (n.d.). ego | Definition & Facts. Retrieved November 4, 2021, from https://www.britannica.com/topic/ego-philosophy-and-psychology

[7] Stangor, C. (2014, October 17). 4.2 Our Brains Control Our Thoughts, Feelings, and Behaviour – Introduction to Psychology – 1st Canadian Edition. Pressbooks. Retrieved November 24, 2021, from

https://opentextbc.ca/introductiontopsychology/chapter/3-2-our-brains-control-our-thoughts-feelings-and-behavior/

[8] Stangor, C. (2014b, October 17). 4.2 Our Brains Control Our Thoughts, Feelings, and Behaviour – Introduction to Psychology – 1st Canadian Edition. Pressbooks. Retrieved November 24, 2021, from https://opentextbc.ca/introductiontopsychology/chapter/3-2-our-brains-control-our-thoughts-feelings-and-behavior/

[9] Chestnut, B. (2013). The Complete Enneagram: 27 Paths to Greater Self-Knowledge (Illustrated ed.). She Writes Press. P. 15

[10] Cron, I. M., & Stabile, S. (2016). The Road Back to You: An Enneagram Journey to Self-Discovery. IVP Books. P. 22-23

[11] Chamine, S. (2012). Positive Intelligence: Why Only 20% of Teams and Individuals Achieve Their True Potential and How You Can Achieve Yours. Greenleaf Book Group Press. P 33-34

[12] Bob Newhart–Stop It. (n.d.). YouTube. Retrieved November 1, 2021, from https://www.youtube.com/watch?v=arPCE3zDRg4

[13] Stanley, A. (2021, January 16). How Not To Be Your Own Worst Enemy, Part 1 – "Pay Attention to the Tension. Apple Podcasts. Retrieved March 9, 2022, from https://podcasts.apple.com/ca/podcast/how-not-to-be-your-own-worst-enemy-part-1-pay-attention/id211872550?i=1000505518238

[14] Stanley, A. (2019, December 29). Winning. Apple Podcasts. Retrieved November 23, 2021, from https://podcasts.apple.com/ca/podcast/north-point-community-church/id262317288?i=1000461028959

[15] Robbins, T. (2019, August 21). Energy Flows Where Attention Goes–Focus & Energy | Tony Robbins. Tonyrobbins.Com. Retrieved November 3, 2021, from https://www.tonyrobbins.com/career-business/where-focus-goes-energy-flows/

[16] Sinek, S., Mead, D., & Docker, P. (2017). Find Your Why: A Practical Guide for Discovering Purpose for You and Your Team (Illustrated ed.). Portfolio. P.74

[17] North Point Community Church. (2018, November 12). Be Rich Part 2 // Andy Stanley & Jeff Foxworthy. YouTube. Retrieved November 24, 2021, from https://www.youtube.com/watch?v=EumEdusJzM8

[18] Stanley, A. (2020). Irresistible: Reclaiming the New that Jesus Unleashed for the World. Zondervan. P. 301

[19] Definition of thankfulness | Cambridge Dictionary. (n.d.). Www. Dictionary.Cambridge.org . Retrieved February 5, 2022, from https://dictionary.cambridge.org/dictionary/english/thankfulness

[20] Definition of fulfill | Dictionary.com. (n.d.). Www.Dictionary. Com. Retrieved November 24, 2021, from https://www.dictionary.com/browse/fulfill

[21] Definition of full | Dictionary.com. (n.d.). Www.Dictionary.Com. Retrieved November 24, 2021, from https://www.dictionary.com/browse/full

[22] Definition of fill | Dictionary.com. (n.d.). Www.Dictionary.Com. Retrieved November 24, 2021, from https://www.dictionary.com/browse/fill

BIBLE REFERENCES

Manufactured by Amazon.ca
Bolton, ON

27239044R00090